Knitting *the*
National
Parks

Knitting the National Parks

63 Easy-to-Follow Designs for Beautiful Beanies Inspired by the US National Parks

Nancy Bates

weldon**owen**

To Scott, Natalie, Caitlin, and Alyson:
my greatest adventure of all.

CONTENTS

INTRODUCTION

The US National Parks draw visitors from around the world. Stop at any scenic overlook in a busy park and you'll likely hear several different languages spoken around you. The reason that visitors flock to these sites is simple: the need to connect with nature is as universal as the need to connect with people. There's something so incredible about standing on land that looks almost the same as it did thousands of years ago and will likely look similar thousands of years from now. As vast and public as these places are, the memories we gain from visiting them are deeply personal and stay in our hearts for years. It could be as simple as seeing fireflies for the first time in the Great Smokies, hearing the nighttime call of loons in Voyageurs, or remembering that Grandpa taught you how to fish in Yosemite. Maybe it was the time you saw bald eagles on a solo trek through Yellowstone, watched a meteor shower with friends in Joshua Tree, or shared an unforgettable view with your family from an observation tower in Hot Springs. Artists, photographers, songwriters, and storytellers have captured and immortalized these beautiful places and personal memories for generations. The time has come for knitters to do the same!

All of the sixty-three designs in this book are as unique as the sixty-three parks that inspired them. You'll find cable stitches turned into trees and cave formations, bobbles turned into coral reefs and treetops, and colorwork galore turned into the jaw-dropping landscapes we all recognize. Page by page, you'll find a range of designs suitable for beginners such as Grand Canyon (pages 122–125) or Capitol Reef (pages 110–113) all the way to more complex patterns such as Lassen Volcanic (pages 201–204) or Badlands (pages 54–57). You'll find the parks and stitches you know and love and the parks and stitches that are new to you. But what I hope you find the most is inspiration. Inspiration to go see that waterfall you've always dreamed of, try a new stitch you originally thought was too difficult, or knit hats for all your park-loving friends. Let the knitting adventure begin, stitch by stitch!

CHOOSING YARN

All the designs in this book, except for Black Canyon of the Gunnison (pages 98–101), call for worsted weight yarn—also referred to as a #4. Worsted weight is warm and cozy, making it a great choice for hats. It's also quick and easy to work with (especially when trying new stitches) and doesn't require a lot of yardage per hat. Because it's durable, washable, and has amazing depth of color, I lean toward using Superwash Merino for most designs. Other wools, wool blends, and acrylics are good choices too. Cotton is not recommended due to its lack of memory—the hat will not keep its shape. Whatever you choose, be sure your yarn feels great and has good stitch definition so that all that stitch work isn't lost in the yarn.

Deciding which color yarn to use is one of the exciting parts of making your own hat. This is when creative decisions are made. Do you want it to look just like mine? Or make it look completely different, so it matches your memories of the park? As an example, my Yosemite beanie depicts a green valley. Maybe you visited Yosemite in the winter when the valley was covered in snow. Try switching some of the green to white. A customer once told me the Everglades Beanie (pages 38–41) reminded her of a lake close to her hometown, so she switched the colors of the trees to orange and created an autumn scene. The textured and layered designs such as Grand Canyon, Capitol Reef, or Bryce Canyon look lovely made with just one or two colors. They don't look like the parks anymore, but they are still beautiful designs, which makes the patterns even more versatile. The color choices are endless! Raid your stash, try something new, or if you'd like to take out the guesswork, purchase one of my handy kits on www.nancybatesdesigns.com. It's all up to you.

GAUGE AND SIZING

Achieving the correct gauge (number of stitches per inch) in your knitting is very important in making sure your hat fits. If you knit tightly, your hat will be smaller. If you knit loosely, your hat will be larger. The hats in this book are designed to be "one size fits most adults" and will fit if you have the correct gauge. Before beginning your chosen design, knit a small swatch (about a 4 in. square) in stockinette stitch (or other stitch as specified in the pattern) with the same yarn and same needle you plan to use for the hat. Block the swatch, let it dry, and then carefully count your stitches against a ruler. Adjust your needles up or down until you get the correct gauge. If you want your hat to fit bigger or smaller, simply go up or down one or two needle sizes (respectively) to achieve your desired fit.

CASTING ON

When choosing a cast-on method, be sure to choose one that is stretchy and suitable for hats. The long-tail cast-on is my preferred method and the one I used throughout this book. It's consistent, simple, neat, and flexible. If you want to experiment with another method, test a sample ribbing first to check for flexibility before continuing with your hat.

WET BLOCKING A HAT

Wet blocking is a technique used to give knitted items a neater, finished appearance. It's especially important in stranded colorwork as it helps relax the stitches and even out the tension. It also rounds out the top of a hat to reduce any unwanted pointiness. It can even help a hat that's slightly too tight fit a little better.

1. Begin by soaking the hat in a small tub or bowl of cool water. Add a little no-rinse wool wash to the water if desired. If you're concerned about color transfer between dark and light colors, add a commercial "color catching" sheet to the water. Attach the ribbing end of the hat to the side of the tub using a large clip, keeping the ribbing just above the water level while the rest of the hat soaks. Leaving the ribbing above the waterline keeps it from stretching out too much. Soak the hat for a few minutes.

2. Carefully lift the hat from the water, supporting it from the bottom to avoid excess stretching. Keep the ribbing toward the top to keep it dry, then gently squeeze out as much water as possible from the hat. Do NOT wring or twist.

3. Roll the hat in a clean, dry towel and gently, but firmly, press down on the towel to remove excess water.

4. Carefully place your hat across an overturned bowl or other rounded object (even a balloon) to dry. Be sure the object is the size you want your finished hat to be. Smooth out any uneven stitches and very gently pull or stretch the hat as needed to remove puckers or make the hat a little bigger. Pat down and shape the crown of the hat, removing any unwanted pointiness. Allow the hat to dry overnight.

Acadia

MAINE

Acadia National Park is known for its beautiful rocky coastlines, spectacular sunrises, and towering granite peaks, as well as its quaint carriage roads and stone bridges. It also boasts miles and miles of trails through gorgeous woodlands and meadows, including this lovely birch-lined section of Jesup Path, near Eagle Lake or Bubble Pond. So often, it's the sweeping, epic views in the parks that capture our hearts. But sometimes, it's the lesser-known pockets of solitude and beauty that seep in and hold on. This beanie uses stranded colorwork to recreate the high contrast look of birch bark, with an optional two-toned pom-pom to represent the leaves.

SIZE

One size fits an average adult size head (approx. 19 in. / 48 cm to 22 in. / 56 cm).

YARN

☐ **A:** Malabrigo Rios, Natural (50 g / 100 yd. / 91 m)

◼ **B:** Malabrigo Rios, Sand Storm (20 g / 40 yd. / 37 m)

◻ **C:** Peekaboo Yarns Merino Worsted, Stornoway (20 g / 40 yd. / 37 m)

Or other worsted weight (#4) yarn in three colors.

Optional Pom-Pom: Peekaboo Yarns Merino Worsted

Colors: Kiwi and Goldenrod (approximately 10 g / 20 yd. / 18 m each)

Or other worsted weight yarn (#4) in two colors.

NEEDLES

- US size 5 / 3.75 mm, 16 in. long circular knitting needles
- US size 7 / 4.5 mm, 16 in. long circular knitting needles
- US size 7 / 4.5 mm double pointed needles (DPNs)

Or sizes needed to obtain gauge.

Continued on next page

- Three stitch markers (two of one color and one of another color)
- Tapestry needle for weaving in ends

GAUGE

With larger needles, approximately 9½ stitches = 2 in. in stockinette stitch.

With color A and smaller circular needles, cast on 96 stitches. Place single color marker and join in the round being careful not to twist stitches.

Work k1, p1 rib pattern for approximately 1½ in. to 2 in.

Switch to larger needles and work chart from right to left beginning on Row 1, bottom right corner. Chart repeats three times around the hat. Use the two remaining stitch markers of another color to mark chart repeats.

Note: In order to avoid long "floats" (strands of yarn on the inside of the hat), do not carry a color more than three to four stitches without twisting the colors around each other in the back of work.

Switch to DPNs when work becomes too small for circular needles.

FINISHING

After Row 47 is complete, cut yarn leaving a 10 in. tail. Using a tapestry needle, weave tail through remaining stitches and pull tightly to close circle. Pull the tail to the inside and weave in all ends.

Using your favorite method, make a pom-pom using green or yellow yarn, or a combination of both. Attach pom-pom to the top of the hat using a tapestry needle.

Block as desired. See page 12 for wet blocking technique.

Go on adventures!

KEY

☐ A

■ B

■ C

☐ Knit
k

◪ Knit 2 Together
k2tog

■ No Stitch

Note: The "no stitch" squares represent the stitches that were lost due to decreases earlier in the project. Do not skip a stitch. Simply treat the squares as if they do not exist.

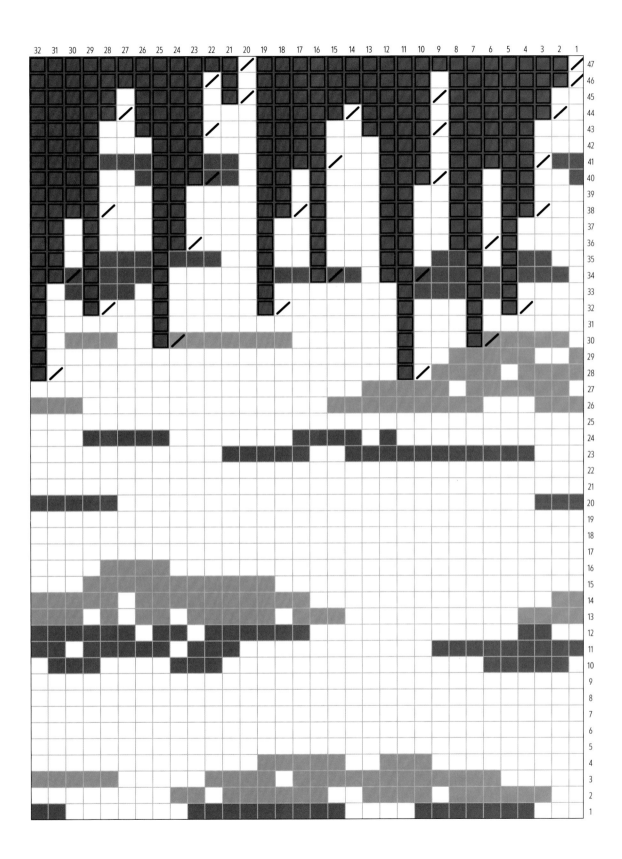

New River Gorge

WEST VIRGINIA

If you're looking for adrenaline-pumping adventures from white water rafting and BASE jumping, to rock climbing and mountain biking, New River Gorge is the place for you! On the flip side, if camping, hiking, and scenic drives are more your style, you'll find those here as well. Spring wildflowers, warm summers, spectacular fall foliage, and snowy winters keep visitors coming year-round. Using four bold colors of nature, images of kayaks, paddles, and the famous New River Gorge Bridge come alive in this blend of stranded colorwork and classic stripes.

SIZE

One size fits an average adult size head (approx. 19 in. / 48 cm to 22 in. / 56 cm).

YARN

A: Stunning String Studio Legacy Worsted, Black Forest (33 g / 66 yd. / 61 m)

B: Malabrigo Rios, Denim (20g / 40 yd. / 37m)

C: Polka Dot Sheep Whitefish Worsted, Stageline (20 g / 40 yd. / 37 m)

D: Stunning String Studio Legacy Worsted, Pine Cone (20 g / 40 yd. / 37 m)

Or other worsted weight yarn (#4) in four colors.

NEEDLES

- US size 5 / 3.75 mm, 16 in. long circular knitting needles
- US size 7 / 4.5 mm, 16 in. long circular knitting needles
- US size 7 / 4.5 mm double pointed needles (DPNs)

Or sizes needed to obtain gauge.

Continued on next page

NOTIONS

- Four stitch markers (three of one color and one of another color)
- Tapestry needle for weaving in ends and adding paddles

GAUGE

With larger needles, approximately 9½ stitches = 2 in. in stockinette stitch.

With color A and smaller circular needles, cast on 96 stitches. Place single color marker and join in the round being careful not to twist stitches. Work in k1 tbl (through back loop), p1 rib pattern for approximately 1½ in.

Switch to larger needles and work chart from right to left beginning on Row 1, bottom right corner. Chart repeats four times around the hat. Use the three remaining stitch markers of another color to mark chart repeats.

Note: In order to avoid long "floats" (strands of yarn on the inside of the hat) do not carry a color more than three to four stitches without twisting the colors around each other in the back of work. Do not pull stitches too tightly or your hat will be too small.

Switch to DPNs when work becomes too small for circular needles.

FINISHING

After Row 45 is complete, cut yarn leaving a 10 in. tail. Using a tapestry needle, weave tail through remaining stitches and pull tightly to close circle. Pull the tail to the inside and weave in all ends.

Block as desired. See page 12 for wet blocking technique.

Paddles (Figure 1): With tapestry needle and color D, add paddles to kayaks using duplicate stitches and freestyle embroidery. Start by adding the duplicate stitch on Row 3. From the middle of this stitch, bring yarn up and over kayak to work duplicate stitch on Row 7. This will create one long strand (straight stitch) over the boat connected by two duplicate stitches. Next, close off the V of the duplicate stitch on Row 7 with a small straight stitch. Add two or three tiny stitches over paddle to "anchor" it to the hat. Lastly, close off the V of duplicate stitch on Row 3. Bring yarn to the back. Weave in ends.

Go on adventures!

Figure 1

KEY

- ■ A
- □ B
- □ C
- ■ D
- □ Knit
  k
- ◿ Knit 2 Together
  k2tog
- ⊡ Duplicate Stitch
  Add duplicate stitching after all
  other knitting is complete
- ⋁ Slip Purlwise with Yarn in Back
  sl wyib
- ■ No Stitch

Note: The "no stitch" squares represent
the stitches that were lost due to decreases
earlier in the project. Do not skip a stitch.
Simply treat these squares as if they do
not exist.

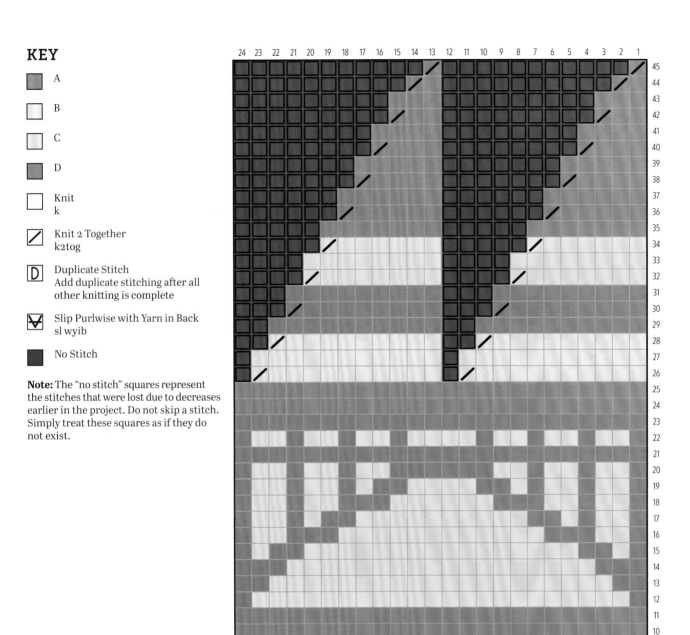

Duplicate Stitches: Add duplicate stitches after all other knitting is complete. In the
meantime, knit these stitches using color B.

Shenandoah

VIRGINIA

With blazing colors of red, orange, yellow, gold, maroon, and purple as far as the eye can see, it's easy to understand why autumn is the most popular time to visit this beautiful park. Even an up-close view of a single leaf can reveal an unexpected kaleidoscope of color. It's an amazing example of the beauty of the changing seasons. This beanie features three different leaf shapes and a simple Fair Isle design in five luscious colors to capture the warmth of the autumnal season.

SIZE

One size fits an average adult size head (approx. 19 in. / 48 cm to 22 in. / 56 cm).

YARN

Aly Bee Workshop Merino Worsted:

- **A:** Black Cherry (25 g / 50 yd. / 46 m)
- **B:** Maple leaf (33 g / 66 yd. / 60 m)
- **C:** Honey Bee (10 g / 20 yd. / 18 m)
- **D:** Spiced Cider (20 g / 40 yd. / 37 m)
- **E:** Cold Brew (20 g / 40 yd. / 37 m)

Or other worsted weight (#4) yarn in five colors.

NEEDLES

- US size 5 / 3.75 mm, 16 in. long circular knitting needles
- US size 7 / 4.5 mm, 16 in. long circular knitting needles
- US size 7 / 4.5 mm double pointed needles (DPNs)

Or sizes needed to obtain gauge.

Continued on next page

THE NORTHEAST REGION   23

NOTIONS

- Three stitch markers (two of one color and one of another color)
- Tapestry needle for weaving in ends

GAUGE

With larger needles, approximately 9½ stitches = 2 in. in stockinette stitch.

With color A and smaller circular needles, cast on 96 stitches. Place single color marker and join in the round being careful not to twist stitches. Work k1, p1 rib pattern for approximately 1½ to 2 in.

Increase row: *k32, M1, repeat from * to end of round— 99 sts total.

Switch to larger needles and work chart from right to left

beginning on Row 1, bottom right corner. Chart repeats three times around the hat. Use the two remaining stitch markers of another color to mark chart repeats.

Note: In order to avoid long "floats" (strands of yarn on the inside of the hat) do not carry a color more than three to four stitches without twisting the colors around each other in the back of work.

Switch to DPNs when work becomes too small for circular needles.

FINISHING

After Row 46 is complete, cut yarn leaving a 10 in. tail. Using a tapestry needle, weave tail through remaining stitches and pull tightly to close circle. Pull the tail to the inside and weave in all ends.

Block as desired. See page 12 for wet blocking technique.

Go on adventures!

KEY

■	A
■	B
☐	C
■	D
■	E
☐	Knit k
◹	Knit 2 Together k2tog
■	No Stitch

Note: The "no stitch" squares represent the stitches that were lost due to decreases earlier in the project. Do not skip a stitch. Simply treat the squares as if they do not exist.

Biscayne

FLORIDA

With 95% of Biscayne's 173,000 acres under water, it's easy to see why this Florida park is so popular with divers, snorkelers, and boaters. Under the beautiful aquamarine waters, visitors can explore a world of coral reefs and colorful fish, shipwrecks, and evidence of pirates. Above the water, mangrove forests and small islands offer up adventures for nature enthusiasts, history buffs, or anyone else who loves a beautiful view in an amazing setting. Inspired by the colorful coral reefs of Biscayne, this design combines a variety of textures and carefully chosen colors to create a hat that's fun to knit and wear.

SIZE

One size fits an average adult size head (approx. 19 in. / 48 cm to 22 in. / 56 cm).

YARN

Peekaboo Yarns Merino Worsted:

- **A:** Biscayne Blue (33 g / 66 yd. / 60 m)
- **B:** Lagoon (20 g / 40 yd. / 37 m)
- **C:** Coral Blush (15 g / 30 yd. / 27 m)
- **D:** Cantaloupe (15 g / 30 yd. / 27 m)
- **E:** Pale Lemondrop (15 g / 30 yd. / 27 m)

Or other worsted weight (#4) yarn in five colors.

NEEDLES

- US size 5 / 3.75 mm, 16 in. long circular knitting needles
- US size 7 / 4.5 mm, 16 in. long circular knitting needles
- US size 7 / 4.5 mm double pointed needles (DPNs)

Or sizes needed to obtain gauge.

Continued on next page

NOTIONS

- Three stitch markers (two of one color and one of another color)
- Tapestry needle for weaving in ends

GAUGE

With larger needles, approximately 9½ stitches = 2 in. in stockinette stitch.

With color A and smaller circular needles, cast on 96 stitches. Place single color marker and join in the round being careful not to twist stitches. Work k2, p2 rib pattern for approximately 1½ to 2 in.

Increase row: *k10, M1. Repeat from * to last 6 stitches. k6— 105 sts total.

Switch to larger needles and work chart from right to left beginning on Row 1, bottom right corner. Chart repeats three times around the hat. Use the two remaining stitch markers of another color to mark chart repeats.

Note: In order to avoid long "floats" (strands of yarn on the inside of the hat) do not carry a color more than three to four stitches without twisting the colors around each other in the back of work.

Switch to DPNs when work becomes too small for circular needles.

FINISHING

After Row 47 is complete, cut yarn leaving a 10 in. tail. Using a tapestry needle, weave tail through remaining stitches and pull tightly to close circle. Pull tail to the inside and weave in all ends.

Block as desired. See page 12 for wet blocking technique.

Go on adventures!

KEY

▨	A
▨	B
▨	C
▨	D
▢	E
⬤	Bobble (p1, k1, p1, k1) into next stitch, then lift 2nd, 3rd, and 4th stitches over first stitch, one at a time.
▢	Knit k
◸	Knit 2 Together k2tog
⊟	Purl p
▨	No Stitch

Note: The "no stitch" squares represent the stitches that were lost due to decreases earlier in the project. Do not skip a stitch. Simply treat the squares as if they do not exist.

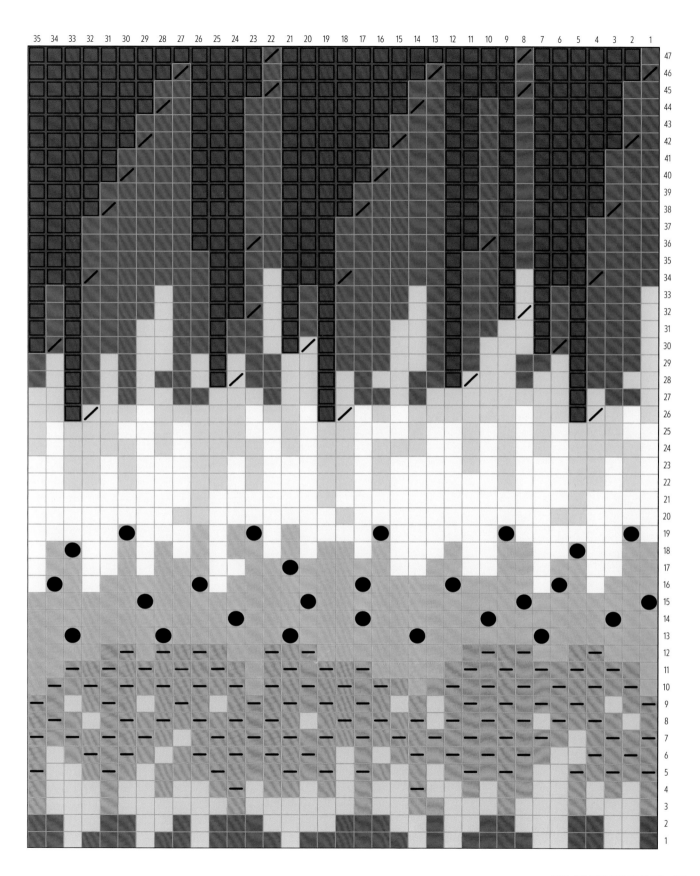

Congaree

SOUTH CAROLINA

A The old-growth bottomland hardwood forest that covers much of Congaree is regularly flooded with waters from the Congaree and Wateree Rivers. These floodwaters not only bring rich nutrients to the trees, but also create a striped appearance on the trunks indicating recent depths of water. In this beanie, lots of texture and cable patterns create a forest of trees embossed against layers of color from the roots to the canopy and the sky above.

SIZE

One size fits an average adult size head (approx. 19 in. / 48 cm to 22 in. / 56 cm).

YARN

☐ **A:** Aly Bee Workshop Merino Worsted, Driftwood (33 g / 66 yd. / 62 m)

☐ **B:** Malabrigo Rios, Yerba (13 g / 25 yd. / 23 m)

☐ **C:** Malabrigo Rios, Ivy (25 g / 50 yd. / 46 m)

☐ **D:** Peekaboo Yarns Merino Worsted, Tide Pool (13 g / 25 yd. / 23 m)

Or other worsted weight (#4) yarn in four colors.

NEEDLES

- US size 5 / 3.75 mm, 16 in. long circular knitting needles
- US size 7 / 4.5 mm, 16 in. long circular knitting needles
- US size 7 / 4.5 mm double pointed needles (DPNs)

Or sizes needed to obtain gauge.

Continued on next page

NOTIONS

- Three stitch markers (two of one color and one of another color)
- Tapestry needle for weaving in ends
- Cable needle (cn)

GAUGE

With larger needles, approximately 9½ stitches = 2 in. in stockinette stitch.

With color A and smaller circular needles, cast on 96 stitches. Place single color marker and join in the round being careful not to twist stitches. Work in rib pattern for approximately 1½ in.

Rib pattern: *k2, p2, k6, p2, k6, p2, k2, p2, k6, p2. Repeat from * two more times.

Switch to larger needles and work chart from right to left beginning on Row 1, bottom right corner. Chart repeats three times around the hat. Use the two remaining stitch markers of another color to mark chart repeats.

Switch to DPNs when work becomes too small for circular needles.

FINISHING

After Row 45 is complete, cut yarn leaving a 10 in. tail. Using a tapestry needle, weave tail through remaining stitches and pull tightly to close circle. Pull tail to the inside and weave in all ends.

Block as desired. See page 12 for wet blocking technique.

Go on adventures!

KEY

A	
B	
C	
D	

1/1 Left Purl Cable
1/1 lpc
Sl 1 to cn, hold in front, p1: k1 from cn

1/1 Right Purl Cable
1/1 rpc
Sl 1 to cn, hold in back, k1: p1 from cn

2/1 Left Purl Cable
2/1 lpc
Sl 2 to cn, hold in front, p1: k2 from cn

2/1 Right Purl Cable
2/1 rpc
Sl 1 to cn, hold in back, k2: p1 from cn

Bobble
(p1, k1, p1, k1) into next stitch, then lift 2nd, 3rd, and 4th stitches up and over first stitch (and off needle), one at a time.

Knit
k

Knit 2 Together
k2tog

Purl
p

Purl 2 Together
p2tog

No Stitch

Note: The "no stitch" squares represent the stitches that were lost due to decreases earlier in the project. Do not skip a stitch. Simply treat these squares as if they do not exist.

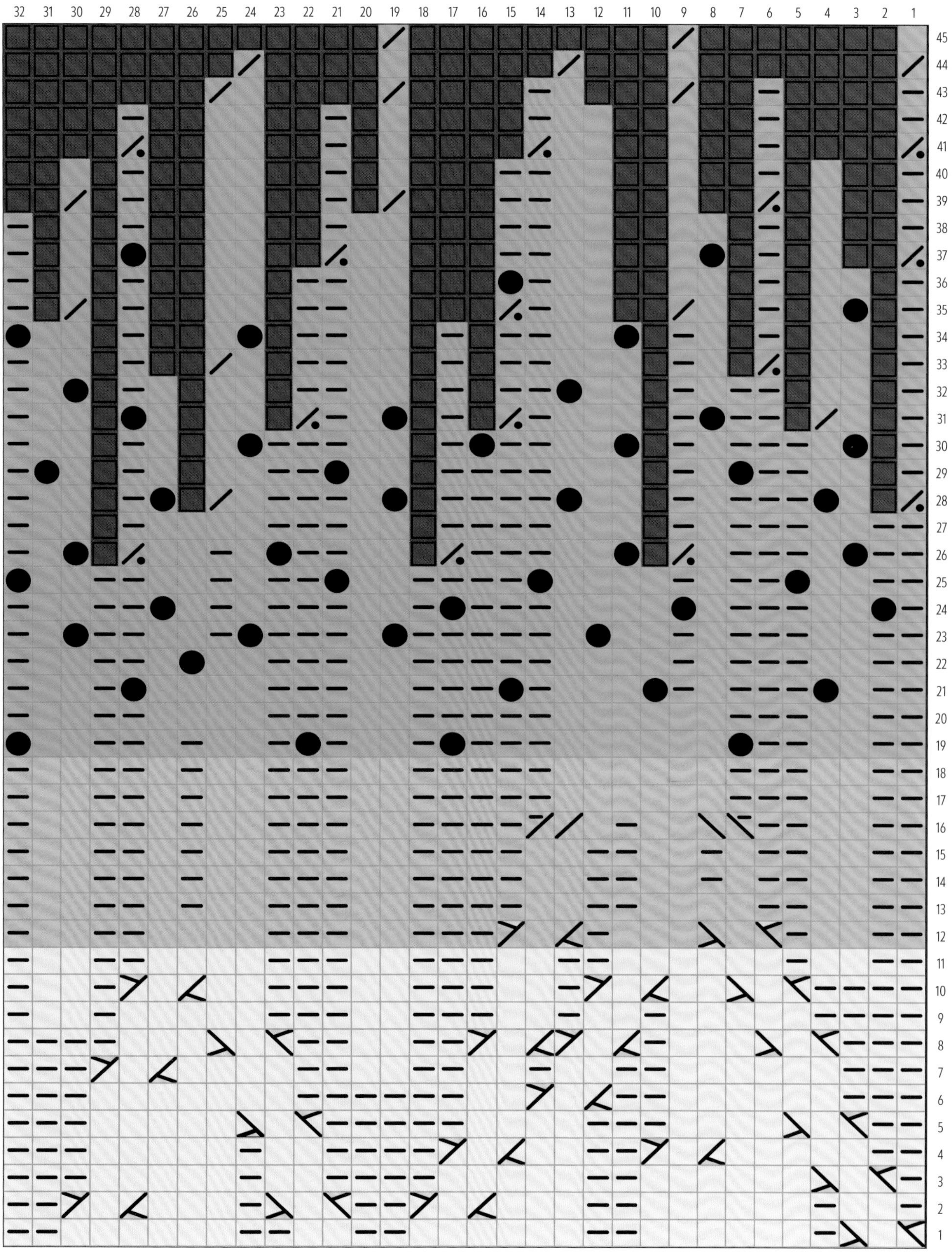
32 31 30 29 28 27 26 25 24 23 22 21 20 19 18 17 16 15 14 13 12 11 10 9 8 7 6 5 4 3 2 1
45 44 43 42 41 40 39 38 37 36 35 34 33 32 31 30 29 28 27 26 25 24 23 22 21 20 19 18 17 16 15 14 13 12 11 10 9 8 7 6 5 4 3 2 1

Dry Tortugas

FLORIDA

A visit to Dry Tortugas, which is 70 miles off the coast of Key West, feels like a step back in time. This remote park encompasses 100 miles of open water with seven small islands, including Garden Key, home of the world famous and historic Fort Jefferson. Using simple stitch techniques, this design takes you from the deep blue and aquamarine waters, to the moat wall and brick fort, up to a clear blue sky. Rows of green represent the grass on the roof while carefully placed decreases hint at the hexagon shape of the fort.

SIZE

One size fits an average adult size head (approx. 19 in. / 48 cm to 22 in. / 56 cm).

YARN

A: Peekaboo Yarns Superwash Merino Worsted, Biscayne Blue (20 g / 40 yd. / 37 m)

B: Aly Bee Workshop Superwash Merino Worsted, Ocean Water (20 g / 40 yd. / 37 m)

C: Malabrigo Rios, Camel (13 g / 25 yd. / 23 m)

D: Peekaboo Yarns Superwash Merino Worsted: Yam (13 g / 25 yd. / 23 m)

E: Malabrigo Rios, Lettuce (13 g / 25 yd. / 23 m)

F: Aly Bee Workshop Superwash Merino Worsted, Glass Slipper (20 g / 40 yd. / 37 m)

Or other worsted weight (#4) yarn in six colors.

NEEDLES

- US size 5 / 3.75 mm, 16 in. long circular knitting needles
- US size 7 / 4.5 mm, 16 in. long circular knitting needles
- US size 7 / 4.5 mm double pointed needles (DPNs)

Or sizes needed to obtain gauge.

Continued on next page

NOTIONS

- Six stitch markers (five of one color and one of another color)
- Tapestry needle for weaving in ends

GAUGE

With larger needles, approximately 9½ stitches = 2 in. in stockinette stitch.

With color A and smaller circular needles, cast on 96 stitches. Place single color marker and join in the round being careful not to twist stitches.

Work k1, p1 rib pattern for approximately 1½ to 2 in.

Increase row: *k15, knit in front and back of next stitch. Repeat from * to end of round—102 sts total.

Switch to larger needles and work chart from right to left beginning on Row 1, bottom right corner. Chart repeats six times around the hat. Use the five remaining stitch markers of another color to mark chart repeats.

Switch to DPNs when work becomes too small for circular needles.

FINISHING

After Row 47 is complete, cut yarn leaving a 10 in. tail. Using a tapestry needle, weave tail through remaining stitches and pull tightly to close circle. Pull tail to the inside and weave in all ends.

Block as desired. See page 12 for wet blocking technique.

Go on adventures!

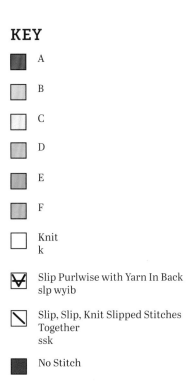

A

B

C

D

E

F

Knit
k

⋎ Slip Purlwise with Yarn In Back
slp wyib

⧄ Slip, Slip, Knit Slipped Stitches
Together
ssk

No Stitch

Note: The "no stitch" squares represent the stitches that were lost due to decreases earlier in the project. Do not skip a stitch. Simply treat the squares as if they do not exist.

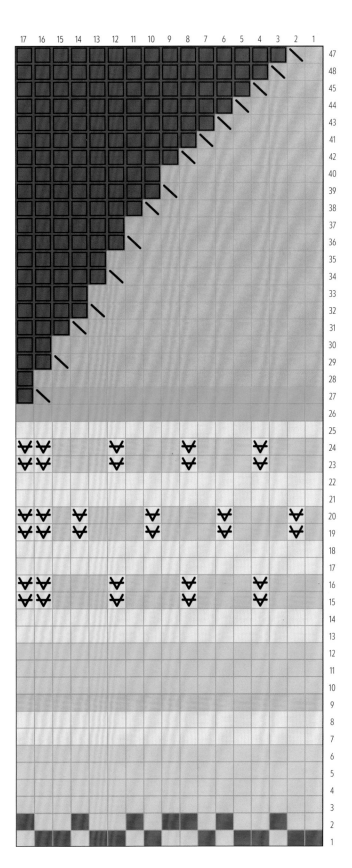

Everglades

FLORIDA

The tangled stilt root system of the mangrove forests growing at the water's edge is one of the most recognizable features of the Everglades. The nearly still water surface creates a mirrored image of sky, clouds, and trees with only the dark soil line to separate reality from reflection. Whether it is worked in the traditional colors of the mangrove forests or something else entirely, the mirror image design of this beanie creates a fun and unusual take on Fair Isle knitting.

SIZE

One size fits an average adult size head (approx. 19 in. / 48 cm to 22 in. / 56 cm).

YARN

- **A:** Peekaboo Yarns Merino Worsted, Everglades Blue (33 g / 66 yd. / 60 m)
- **B:** Malabrigo Rios, Natural (20 g / 40 yd. / 37 m)
- **C:** Malabrigo Rios, Lettuce (25 g / 50 yd. / 46 m)
- **D:** Cascade Yarns 220 Superwash Effects, Graphite (13 g / 25 yd. / 23 m)
- **E:** Malabrigo Rios, Sandstorm (13 g / 25 yd. / 23 m)

Or other worsted weight (#4) yarn in five colors.

NEEDLES

- US size 5 / 3.75 mm, 16 in. long circular knitting needles
- US size 7 / 4.5 mm, 16 in. long circular knitting needles
- US size 7 / 4.5 mm double pointed needles (DPNs)

Or sizes needed to obtain gauge.

Continued on next page

NOTIONS

- Three stitch markers (two of one color and one of another color)
- Tapestry needle for weaving in ends

GAUGE

With larger needles, approximately 9½ stitches = 2 in. in stockinette stitch.

FINISHING

After Row 44 is complete, cut yarn leaving a 10 in. tail. Using a tapestry needle, weave tail through remaining stitches and pull tightly to close circle. Pull the tail to the inside and weave in all ends.

Block as desired. See page 12 for wet blocking technique.

Go on adventures!

KEY

▨	A
☐	B
▨	C
▨	D
■	E
☐	Knit k
◪	Knit 2 Together k2tog
■	No Stitch

Note: The "no stitch" squares represent the stitches that were lost due to decreases earlier in the project. Do not skip a stitch. Simply treat the squares as if they do not exist.

With color A and smaller circular needles, cast on 96 stitches. Place single color marker and join in the round being careful not to twist stitches. Work k1, p1 rib pattern for approximately 1½ to 2 in.

Increase row: *k31, (k in front and back of next stitch) three times—99 sts total.

Switch to larger needles and work chart from right to left beginning on Row 1, bottom right corner. Chart repeats three times around the hat. Use the two remaining stitch markers of another color to mark chart repeats.

Note: In order to avoid long "floats" (strands of yarn on the inside of the hat) do not carry a color more than three to four stitches without twisting the colors around each other in the back of work.

Switch to DPNs when work becomes too small for circular needles.

Great Smoky Mountains

NORTH CAROLINA/TENNESSEE

An up-close visit to the Great Smoky Mountains reveals a rugged and beautiful landscape of thundering waterfalls, clear streams, and abundant wildlife. But when viewed from a distance, there's even more to behold. This vast and ancient range of tree-covered mountains is a study in subtle texture and gradient hues, while the enveloping fog visually softens its landscape. This beanie uses a variety of textured stitch patterns separated by narrow bands of stockinette stitch. The slight "fuzziness" of the alpaca fibers "visually softens the landscape" of the beanie and is reminiscent of the namesake haze of the park.

SIZE

One size fits an average adult size head (approx. 19 in. / 48 cm to 22 in. / 56 cm).

YARN

Peekaboo Yarns Alpaca/Merino Worsted:

- **A:** Capri Blue (50 g / 100 yd. / 91 m)
- **B:** Light Blue (25 g / 50 yd. / 46 m)
- **C:** Cadet Gray (25 g / 50 yd. / 46 m)

Or other worsted weight yarn (#4) in three colors. Choosing an alpaca or alpaca/wool blend will create the "haziness" of the Great Smoky Mountains.

NEEDLES

- US size 5 / 3.75 mm, 16 in. long circular knitting needles
- US size 7 / 4.5 mm, 16 in. long circular knitting needles
- US size 7 / 4.5 mm double pointed needles (DPNs)

Or sizes needed to obtain gauge.

Continued on next page

NOTIONS

- Four stitch markers (three of one color and one of another color)
- Tapestry needle for weaving in ends

GAUGE

With larger needles, approximately 9½ stitches = 2 in. in stockinette stitch.

With color A and smaller circular needles, cast on 96 stitches. Place single color marker and join in the round being careful not to twist stitches. Work in k1, p1 rib pattern for approximately 1½ in.

Switch to larger needles and work chart from right to left beginning on Row 1, bottom right corner. Chart repeats four times around the hat. Use the three remaining stitch markers of another color to mark chart repeats.

Switch to DPNs when work becomes too small for circular needles.

FINISHING

After Row 45 is complete, cut yarn leaving a 10 in. tail. Using a tapestry needle, weave tail through remaining stitches and pull tightly to close circle. Pull the tail to the inside and weave in all ends.

Block as desired. See page 12 for wet blocking technique.

Go on adventures!

KEY

■	A
▨	B
▨	C
☐	Knit k
╱	Knit 2 Together k2tog
Ⓜ	Make One Purlwise M1P Bringing needle from front to back, lift strand between stitch just worked and the next stitch. Purl into the back of this strand.
⊟	Purl p
╱•	Purl 2 Together p2tog
◣³	Purl 3, Pass One Over p3,p1o Purl 3. Pass first purl stitch over remaining 2 and off of needle. 2 stitches remaining.
■	No Stitch

Note: The "no stitch" squares represent the stitches that were lost due to decreases earlier in the project. Do not skip a stitch. Simply treat the squares as if they do not exist.

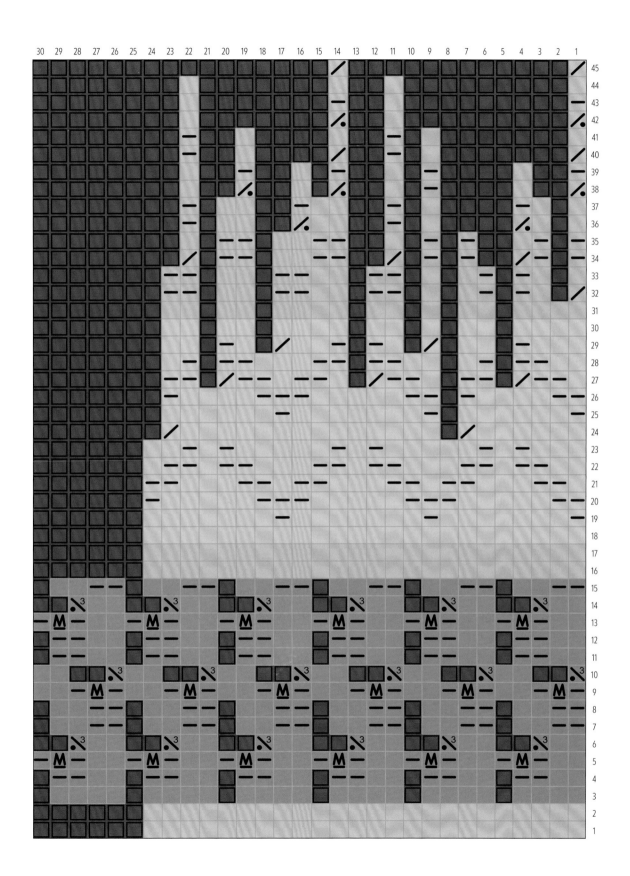

Mammoth Cave

KENTUCKY

In Kentucky, beneath nearly 53,000 acres of woods, river valleys, and rolling hills, lies the largest cave system in the world. With massive individual caverns and over 400 miles of passageways mapped so far, this park has earned its name. Visitors of all ages can walk next to an underground river, gaze upon beautiful cave formations, wonder at archaeological finds, scramble up and down hills, and even experience total darkness. Using only two colors, this design begins with an easy-to-knit pattern representing the dozens of stairways found in the park. A simple band of stockinette stitch leads into randomly placed bobbles reminiscent of the calcite and gypsum formations found on the ceiling of the famous Snowball Room.

SIZE

One size fits an average adult size head (approx. 19 in. / 48 cm to 22 in. / 56 cm).

YARN

A: Malabrigo Rios, Glitter (50 g / 100 yd. / 91 m)

B: Malabrigo Rios, Fog (50 g / 100 yd. / 91 m)

Or other worsted weight yarn (#4) in two colors.

NEEDLES

- US size 5 / 3.75 mm, 16 in. long circular knitting needles
- US size 7 / 4.5 mm, 16 in. long circular knitting needles
- US size 7 / 4.5 mm double pointed needles (DPNs)

Or sizes needed to obtain gauge.

NOTIONS

- Four stitch markers (three of one color and one of another color)
- Tapestry needle for weaving in ends

GAUGE

With larger needles, approximately 9½ stitches = 2 in. in stockinette stitch.

With color A and smaller circular needles, cast on 96 stitches. Place single color marker and join in the round being careful not to twist stitches. Work in k1 tbl (through back loop), p1 pattern for approximately 1½ in.

Switch to larger needles and work chart from right to left beginning on Row 1, bottom right corner. Chart repeats four times around the hat. Use the three remaining stitch markers of another color to mark chart repeats.

Note: In order to avoid long "floats" (strands of yarn on the inside of the hat) do not carry a color more than three to four stitches without twisting the colors around each other in the back of work. Do not pull stitches too tightly or your hat will be too small.

Switch to DPNs when work becomes too small for circular needles.

FINISHING

After Row 45 is complete, cut yarn leaving a 10 in. tail. Using a tapestry needle, weave tail through remaining stitches and pull tightly to close circle. Pull the tail to the inside and weave in all ends.

Block as desired. See page 12 for wet blocking technique.

Go on adventures!

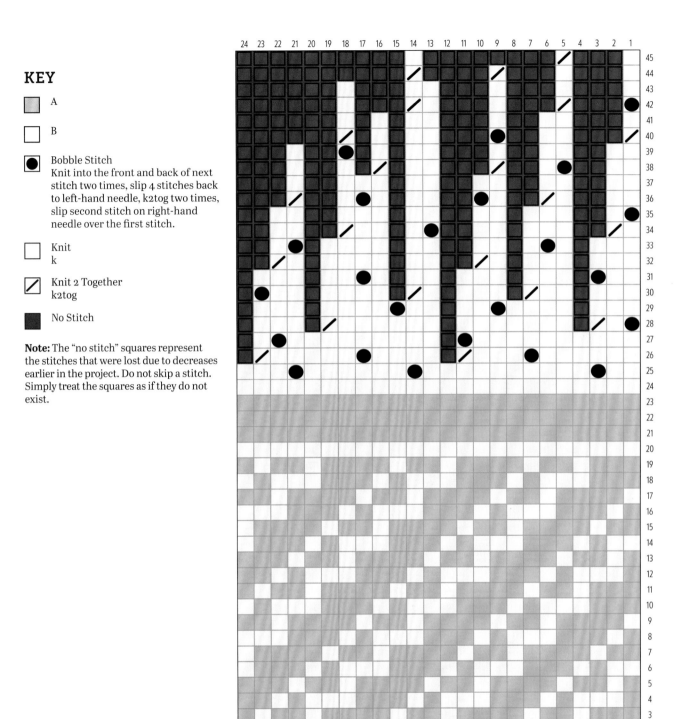

KEY

- A
- B
- Bobble Stitch
  Knit into the front and back of next stitch two times, slip 4 stitches back to left-hand needle, k2tog two times, slip second stitch on right-hand needle over the first stitch.
- Knit
  k
- Knit 2 Together
  k2tog
- No Stitch

Note: The "no stitch" squares represent the stitches that were lost due to decreases earlier in the project. Do not skip a stitch. Simply treat the squares as if they do not exist.

Virgin Islands

VIRGIN ISLANDS

No other setting conjures up images of a tropical paradise quite like the white sand beaches, palm trees, and crystal blue waters of the Virgin Islands. Add in 3,000 years of human history, trails through diverse forests, spectacular snorkeling with sea life galore and you have a tropical adventurer's dream. No wonder this park attracts visitors from around the world! Beginning with a band of lightly textured bougainvillea in the foreground, this design evokes that paradise. With a little imagination, you can almost feel the gentle tropical breeze.

SIZE

One size fits an average adult size head (approx. 19 in. / 48 cm to 22 in. / 56 cm).

YARN

A: Western Sky Knits Merino 17 Worsted, Jasmine (25 g / 50 yd. / 46 m)

B: Malabrigo Rios, Natural (13 g / 25 yd. / 23 m)

C: Malabrigo Rios, Sand Storm (13 g / 25 yd. / 23 m)

D: Aly Bee Workshop Merino Worsted, Ocean Water (13 g / 25 yd. / 23 m)

E: Peekaboo Yarns Merino Worsted, Biscayne Blue (13 g / 25 yd. / 23 m)

F: Aly Bee Workshop Merino Worsted, Glass Slipper (20 g / 40 yd. / 37 m)

G: Forbidden Fiber Co Gluttony Worsted, Gillyweed (20 g / 40 yd. / 37 m)

Or other worsted weight (#4) yarn in seven colors.

NEEDLES

- US size 5 / 3.75 mm, 16 in. long circular knitting needles
- US size 7 / 4.5 mm, 16 in. long circular knitting needles
- US size 7 / 4.5 mm double pointed needles (DPNs)

Or sizes needed to obtain gauge.

Continued on next page

NOTIONS

- Three stitch markers (two of one color and one of another color)
- Tapestry needle for weaving in ends

GAUGE

With larger needles, approximately 9½ stitches = 2 in. in stockinette stitch.

With color A and smaller circular needles, cast on 96 stitches. Place single color marker and join in the round being careful not to twist stitches. Work k1, p1 rib pattern for approximately 1½ to 2 in.

Increase row: *k31, knit in front and back of next stitch. Repeat from * to end of round. 3 increases made—99 sts total.

Switch to larger needles and work chart from right to left beginning on Row 1, bottom right corner. Chart repeats three times around the hat. Use the two remaining stitch markers of another color to mark chart repeats.

Note: In order to avoid long "floats" (strands of yarn on the inside of the hat) do not carry a color more than three to four stitches without twisting the colors around each other in the back of work.

Switch to DPNs when work becomes too small for circular needles.

FINISHING

After Row 45 is complete, cut yarn leaving a 10 in. tail. Using a tapestry needle, weave tail through remaining stitches and pull tightly to close circle. Pull the tail to the inside and weave in all ends.

Block as desired. See page 12 for wet blocking technique.

Go on adventures!

KEY

■	A
□	B
▨	C
■	D
■	E
□	F
▨	G
●	Bobble (p1, k1, p1) into next stitch, then lift 2nd and 3rd stitches over first stitch, one at a time.
□	Knit k
╱	Knit 2 Together k2tog
⊻	Slip Purlwise with Yarn in Back sl wyib
■	No Stitch

Note: The "no stitch" squares represent the stitches that were lost due to decreases earlier in the project. Do not skip a stitch. Simply treat the squares as if they do not exist.

Badlands

SOUTH DAKOTA

The Badlands are a perfect example of the rugged beauty that millions of years of geologic activity, rain, and wind can create. The colorful, fossil-rich layers and weathered formations reveal the history of a land transformed from ancient inland seas and waterways to what we see today. This beanie uses stranded colorwork and crossover stitches to represent both the striped layers and the distinct pointed formations. The Badlands colorway was inspired by dust swirling up into the blue sky.

SIZE

One size fits an average adult size head (approx. 19 in. / 48 cm to 22 in. / 56 cm).

YARN

Big Sky Yarn Co. Merino Worsted:

A: Tennessee Whiskey (50 g / 100 yd. / 91 m)

B: Badlands (50 g / 100 yd. / 91 m)

Or other worsted weight yarn (#4) in two colors.

NEEDLES

- US size 5 / 3.75 mm, 16 in. long circular knitting needles
- US size 7 / 4.5 mm, 16 in. long circular knitting needles
- US size 7 / 4.5 mm double pointed needles (DPNs)

Or sizes needed to obtain gauge.

NOTIONS

- Three stitch markers (two of one color and one of another color)
- Tapestry needle for weaving in ends

GAUGE

With larger needles, approximately 9½ stitches = 2 in. in stockinette stitch.

With color A and smaller circular needles, cast on 96 stitches. Place single color marker and join in the round being careful not to twist stitches. Work in k1, p1 rib pattern for approximately 1½ in.

Increase row: *k11, M1, k11, M1, k10, M1. Repeat from * around—105 sts total.

Switch to larger needles and work chart from right to left beginning on Row 1, bottom right corner. Chart will repeat three times around the hat. Use the two remaining stitch markers of another color to mark chart repeats.

Note: In order to avoid long "floats" (strands of yarn on the inside of the hat) do not carry a color more than three to four stitches without twisting the colors around each other in the back of work. Do NOT pull your floats too tightly or your hat will be too small. Be sure to spread out stitches on your right needle every five stitches or so to help avoid pulling too tightly.

Switch to DPNs when work becomes too small for circular needles.

CROSSOVER STITCHES HELPFUL HINTS

- Be sure to keep stitches in their original order while working crossovers on the left needle. As you slide the stitches off, they will magically trade places.

- Give your yarn a gentle tug as needed after each crossover to even out stitches. Keep watching tension across all stitches. Don't pull too tightly.

- Where you see the crossover symbols in dark brown, work BOTH the first and second stitch of the crossover in color A.

- Crossover stitches may seem awkward at first, but you will quickly get used to them.

SPECIAL INSTRUCTIONS FOR ROW 20

Work row as shown until last stitch of chart repeat. Slide this stitch to right needle. Remove marker, place stitch back on left needle and work right leaning crossover. Place color B stitch back on left needle. Replace marker. Slide that same stitch back to right needle. This stitch now becomes the first (completed) stitch of next chart repeat.

Note: For second and third chart repeats, the first stitch in the row is now color B (not A as shown on chart). At the end of the round, this last stitch will become the first (completed) stitch of Row 21. Work remainder of Row 21 and the rest of the chart as indicated.

SPECIAL INSTRUCTIONS FOR ROW 26

Work row as shown until last stitch of chart repeat. Slide this stitch to right needle. Remove marker, place stitch back on left needle and work right leaning crossover. Place color B stitch back on left needle. Replace marker. Slide that same stitch back to right needle. This stitch now becomes the first (completed) stitch of next chart repeat. At the end of the round, this last stitch will become the first (completed) stitch of Row 27. Work remainder of Row 27 and the rest of the chart as shown.

FINISHING

After Row 47 is complete, cut yarn leaving a 10 in. tail. Using a tapestry needle, weave tail through remaining stitches and pull tightly to close circle. Pull the tail to the inside and weave in all ends.

With all the crossover stitches and colorwork in this design, your hat will need wet blocking to smooth out the fabric. See page 12 for wet blocking technique.

Go on adventures!

KEY

▨ A	
▢ B	

▧▧ **Right Leaning Crossover**
With color A, skip 1st stitch and knit into front of 2nd stitch. Drop color A, pick up color B and knit into 1st stitch. Slide both stitches off left needle.

▧▧ **Left Leaning Crossover**
With color B, skip next stitch and knit into back loop of 2nd stitch. Drop color B, pick up color A and knit into 1st stitch. Slide both stitches off left needle.

▢ **Knit**
k

◪ **Knit 2 Together**
k2tog

▨ **Slip Purlwise with Yarn in Back**
sl wyib

■ **No Stitch**

Note: The "no stitch" squares represent the stitches that were lost due to decreases earlier in the project. Do not skip a stitch. Simply treat the squares as if they do not exist.

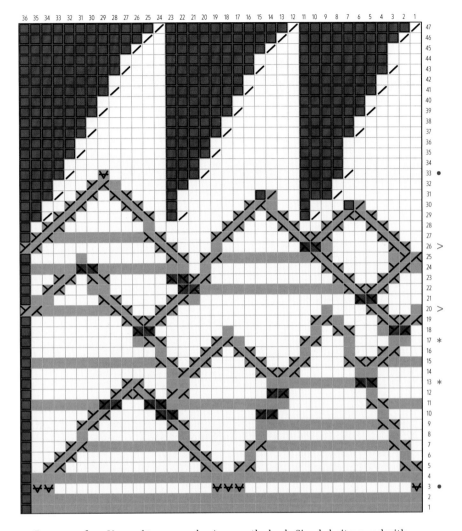

- • **Rows 3 and 33:** No need to carry color A across the back. Simply knit around with color B and slip color A where indicated.

- ✳ **Rows 13 and 17:** To create a smoother transition of stripes between rounds (jog-less stripes), before beginning the round, use your right needle to lift the stitch below the first stitch of the left needle up onto the left needle. Knit these two stitches together.

- > **Rows 20 and 26:** See special instructions for these rows.

Cuyahoga Valley

OHIO

The Cuyahoga River is the heart of Cuyahoga Valley National Park. The famous Towpath Trail running alongside this river was once used by mules, oxen, and horses as they towed boats up the river through the historic Ohio and Erie Canal with ropes. Today, this trail includes nearly 20 miles of mostly flat trails for hikers and bicyclists within the park and extends for many more miles outside of the park. It's lovely at any time of year, but especially beautiful in autumn as the leaves turn to shades of gold and orange. This beanie features mini bobbles to add subtle texture to the foliage of the trees, while the splashes of color in Forest Path depict the fallen leaves on both sides of the river.

SIZE

One size fits an average adult size head (approx. 19 in. / 48 cm to 22 in. / 56 cm).

YARN

Peekaboo Yarns Superwash Merino Worsted:

A: Forest Path (33 g / 66 yd. / 60 m)

B: Warm Brown (20 g / 40 yd. / 37 m)

C: Tide Pool (25 g / 50 yd. / 46 m)

D: Cuyahoga Foliage (25 g / 50 yd. / 46 m)

Or other worsted weight (#4) yarn in four colors.

NEEDLES

- US size 5 / 3.75 mm, 16 in. long circular knitting needles
- US size 7 / 4.5 mm, 16 in. long circular knitting needles
- US size 7 / 4.5 mm double pointed needles (DPNs)

Or sizes needed to obtain gauge.

Continued on next page

NOTIONS

- Four stitch markers (three of one color and one of another color)
- Tapestry needle for weaving in ends

GAUGE

With larger needles, approximately 9½ stitches = 2 in. in stockinette stitch.

With color A and smaller circular needles, cast on 96 stitches. Place single color marker and join in the round being careful not to twist stitches.

Work k2, p2 rib pattern for approximately 1½ in. to 2 in.

Increase row: *k24, M1. Repeat from * around—100 sts total.

Switch to larger needles and work chart from right to left beginning on Row 1, bottom right corner. Chart repeats four times around the hat. Use the three remaining stitch markers of another color to mark chart repeats.

Note: To avoid long "floats" (strands of yarn on the inside of the hat) do not carry a color more than three to four stitches without twisting the colors around each other in the back of work.

Switch to DPNs when work becomes too small for circular needles.

Helpful Hint: If needed, give your mini bobbles a little push from behind and a slight tug from the front to bring the texture to the right side of the hat.

FINISHING

After Row 45 is complete, cut yarn leaving a 10 in. tail. Using a tapestry needle, weave tail through remaining stitches and pull tightly to close circle. Pull the tail to the inside and weave in all ends.

Block as desired. See page 12 for wet blocking technique.

Go on adventures!

KEY

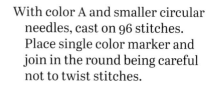

▨	A
▨	B
▨	C
☐	D
●	Mini Bobble (k1, p1, k1) into next stitch, then lift the 2nd and 3rd stitches over first stitch, one at a time.
☐	Knit k
◪	Knit 2 Together k2tog
◼	No Stitch

Note: The "no stitch" squares represent the stitches that were lost due to decreases earlier in the project. Do not skip a stitch. Simply treat the squares as if they do not exist.

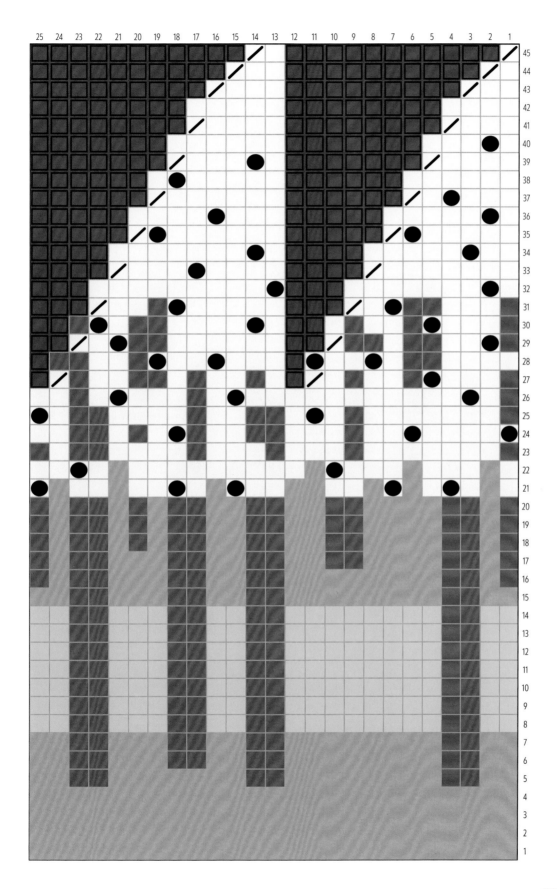

Gateway Arch

MISSOURI

The iconic Gateway Arch commemorates St. Louis's role in the westward expansion of the United States during the nineteenth century. At 630 feet tall, the arch is covered in dozens of stainless-steel panels that gleam in the sun and create an interesting checkerboard pattern. For more than five decades, millions of families have posed for souvenir photos at the base of this impressive monument. Using four different shades of silvers and grays, this beanie recreates the subtle rectangle pattern of the arch while simple embroidered stick figures pose for a photo at the base.

SIZE

One size fits an average adult size head (approx. 19 in. / 48 cm to 22 in. / 56 cm).

YARN

A: Malabrigo Rios, Ivy. Not shown on chart (20 g / 40 yds / 36.5 m)

B: Peekaboo Yarns Merino Worsted, Classic Silver (20 g / 40 yds / 36.5 m)

C: Peekaboo Yarns Merino Worsted, French Silver (20 g / 40 yds / 36.5 m)

D: Peekaboo Yarns Merino Worsted, Graceful Grey (20 g / 40 yds / 36.5 m)

E: Peekaboo Yarns Merino Worsted, Silverstone (20 g / 40 yds / 36.5 m)

Or other worsted weight yarn (#4) in five colors.

Optional: A few yards of any color yarn for embroidering stick figures

NEEDLES

- US size 5 / 3.75 mm, 16 in. long circular knitting needles
- US size 8 / 5 mm, 16 in. long circular knitting needles
- US size 8 / 5 mm double pointed needles (DPNs)

Or sizes needed to obtain gauge.

Continued on next page

NOTIONS

- Three stitch markers (two of one color and one of another color)
- Tapestry needle for weaving in ends and embroidering stick figures

GAUGE

With larger needles, approximately 9½ stitches = 2 in. in stockinette stitch, blocked.

Note: If you already know you are a tight knitter, go up one needle size for both the ribbing and the body of the hat.

With color A and smaller circular needles, cast on 96 stitches. Place single color marker and join in the round being careful not to twist stitches. Work in k1, p1 rib pattern for approximately 1½ in.

Increase row: Switch to larger needles *k31, knit in front and back of next stitch. Repeat from * to end of round—99 sts total.

Switch to larger needles and work chart from right to left beginning on Row 1, bottom right corner. Chart will repeat three times around the hat. Use the two remaining stitch markers of another color to mark chart repeats.

Note: In order to avoid long "floats" (strands of yarn on the inside of the hat) do not carry a color more than three to four stitches without twisting the colors around each other in the back of work. Do NOT pull your floats too tightly or your hat will be too small. Be sure to spread out your stitches on your right needle every five stitches or so to help avoid pulling too tightly.

Switch to DPNs when work becomes too small for circular needles.

FINISHING

After Row 45 is complete, cut yarn leaving a 10 in. tail. Using a tapestry needle, weave tail through remaining stitches and pull tightly to close circle. Pull the tail to the inside and weave in all ends.

Block as desired. See page 12 for wet blocking technique.

Optional: After blocking is complete, use simple embroidery stitches and any color yarn to add stick figures to the hat as desired. I used straight stitches for the bodies and French knots for the heads. You can add one person, your whole family, or even an entire line of people all around the hat. It's up to you!

Go on adventures!

KEY

☐	B
▨	C
▨	D
☐	E
☐	Knit k
◺	Knit 2 Together k2tog
■	No Stitch

Note: The "no stitch" squares represent the stitches that were lost due to decreases earlier in the project. Do not skip a stitch. Simply treat the squares as if they do not exist.

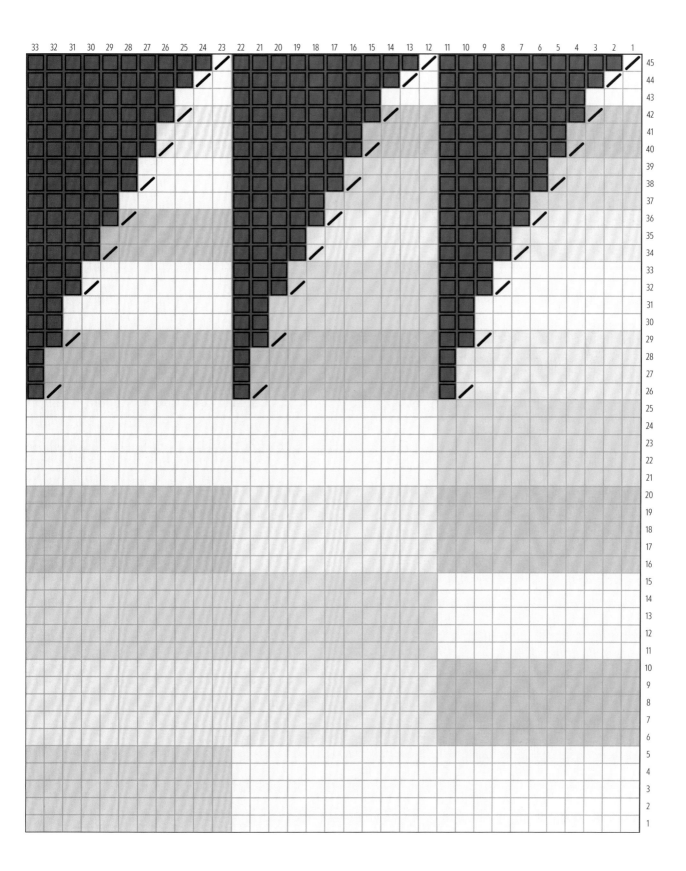

Hot Springs

ARKANSAS

The hot and cold thermal springs of this tiny park in Arkansas have been visited by humans for centuries. As stories of the "healing waters" spread in the early 1800s, an entire town with multiple bathhouses was built. The area became known as the "American Spa." It wasn't long before visitors came from around the country to relax in the spring water and hike the surrounding hillsides—just as they do today. Using six colors and simple stranded knitting, this beanie features the historic Bath House Row surrounded by hedges, walkways, trees, and hillsides.

SIZE

One size fits an average adult size head (approx. 19 in. / 48 cm to 22 in. / 56 cm).

YARN

☐ **A:** Peekaboo Yarns Merino Worsted, Classic Silver (20 g / 40 yds / 37 m)

☐ **B:** Malabrigo Rios, Lettuce (20 g / 40 yds / 37 m)

☐ **C:** Malabrigo Rios, Natural (17 g / 35 yds / 32 m)

■ **D:** Stunning String Studio Legacy Worsted, Charcoal (17 g / 35 yds / 32 m)

☐ **E:** Malabrigo Rios, Ivy (17 g / 35 yds / 32 m)

☐ **F:** Aly Bee Workshop Merino Worsted, Glass Slipper (20 g / 40 yds / 37 m)

Or other worsted weight yarn (#4) in six colors.

NEEDLES

- US size 5 / 3.75 mm, 16 in. long circular knitting needles
- US size 7 / 4.5 mm, 16 in. long circular knitting needles
- US size 7 / 4.5 mm double pointed needles (DPNs)

Or sizes needed to obtain gauge.

Continued on next page

NOTIONS

- Three stitch markers (two of one color and one of another color)
- Tapestry needle for weaving in ends, duplicate stitching, and embroidery

GAUGE

With larger needles, approximately 9½ stitches = 2 in. in stockinette stitch, blocked.

With color A and smaller circular needles, cast on 96 stitches. Place single color marker and join in the round being careful not to twist stitches. Work in k1, p1 rib pattern for approximately 1½ in.

Switch to larger needles and work chart from right to left beginning on Row 1, bottom right corner. Chart repeats three times around the hat. Use the two remaining stitch markers of another color to mark chart repeats.

Note: In order to avoid long "floats" (strands of yarn on the inside of the hat) do not carry a color more than three to four stitches without twisting the colors around each other in the back of work. Do NOT pull your floats too tightly or your hat will be too small. Be sure to spread out your stitches on your right needle every five stitches or so to help avoid pulling too tightly.

Switch to DPNs when work becomes too small for circular needles.

FINISHING

After Row 45 is complete, cut yarn leaving a 10 in. tail. Using a tapestry needle, weave tail through remaining stitches and pull tightly to close circle. Pull the tail to the inside and weave in all ends.

Block as desired. See page 12 for wet blocking technique.

Backstitch Embroidery and Duplicate Stitching: After blocking is complete, use a tapestry needle and color D to embroider lines between buildings using simple backstitch. The lines help to define the structures as separate buildings. As you work your way around the hat, add in the upper windows using duplicate stitch where indicated on chart.

Go on adventures!

KEY

☐	A
☐	B
☐	C
☐	D
☐	E
☐	F
◹	Knit 2 Together k2tog
ᴅ	Duplicate Stitch Work duplicate stitches after all other knitting is complete.
⊟	Purl p
⋁	Slip Purlwise with Yarn in Back sl wyib
■	No Stitch

Note: The "no stitch" squares represent the stitches that were lost due to decreases earlier in the project. Do not skip a stitch. Simply treat the squares as if they do not exist.

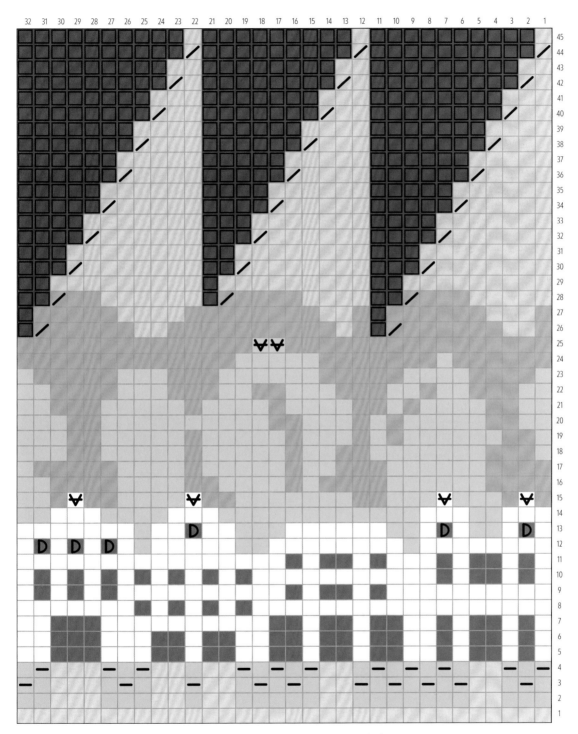

Duplicate Stitch "D": Work duplicate stitches using color D where indicated after all knitting is complete. In the meantime, knit these stitches using color C.

Slipped Stitches Row 15: No need to carry color C across back of work on this row. Knit with colors B and E as shown and then slip color C where indicated.

Slipped Stitches Row 25: No need to carry color B across back of work on this row. Knit with color E across row and then slip color B where indicated.

Indiana Dunes

INDIANA

From kite flying and sandcastle building on the shore of Lake Michigan to hiking and camping in nearby prairies and forests, Indiana Dunes National Park has much to offer anyone looking for outdoor adventures. From fall foliage to spring wildflowers, every season brings something new to explore. Even the cold winters bring activities such as skiing and snowshoeing. With the subdued colors of a lazy summer day, this design features wooden boardwalk fences, grassy dunes, and gentle waves splashing against the shore.

SIZE

One size fits an average adult size head (approx. 19 in. / 48 cm to 22 in. / 56 cm).

YARN

A: Aly Bee Workshop Merino Worsted, Prickly pear (25 g / 50 yd. / 46 m)

B: Malabrigo Rios, Ivory (13 g / 25 yd. / 23 m)

C: Malabrigo Rios, Camel (13 g / 25 yd. / 23 m)

D: Stunning String Studio Legacy Worsted, Big Sky (33 g / 66 yd. / 60 m)

E: Malabrigo Rios, Natural (13 g / 25 yd. / 23 m)

Or other worsted weight yarn (#4) in five colors.

NEEDLES

- US size 5 / 3.75 mm, 16 in. long circular knitting needles
- US size 7 / 4.5 mm, 16 in. long circular knitting needles
- US size 7 / 4.5 mm double pointed needles (DPNs)

Or sizes needed to obtain gauge.

Continued on next page

NOTIONS

- Three stitch markers (two of one color and one of another color)
- Tapestry needle for weaving in ends

GAUGE

With larger needles, approximately 9½ stitches = 2 in. in stockinette stitch, blocked.

With color A and smaller circular needles, cast on 96 stitches. Place single color marker and join in the round being careful not to twist stitches. Work in k1, p1 rib pattern for approximately 1½ in.

Switch to larger needles and work chart from right to left beginning on Row 1, bottom right corner. Chart repeats three times around the hat. Use the two remaining stitch markers of another color to mark chart repeats

Switch to DPNs when work becomes too small for circular needles.

FINISHING

After Row 45 is complete, cut yarn leaving a 10 in. tail. Using a tapestry needle, weave tail through remaining stitches and pull tightly to close circle. Pull the tail to the inside and weave in all ends.

Block as desired. See page 12 for wet blocking technique.

Go on adventures!

KEY

▨	A
▨	B
▨	C
▨	D
☐	E
☐	Knit k
◨	Knit 2 Together k2tog
▨	No Stitch

Note: The "no stitch" squares represent the stitches that were lost due to decreases earlier in the project. Do not skip a stitch. Simply treat the squares as if they do not exist.

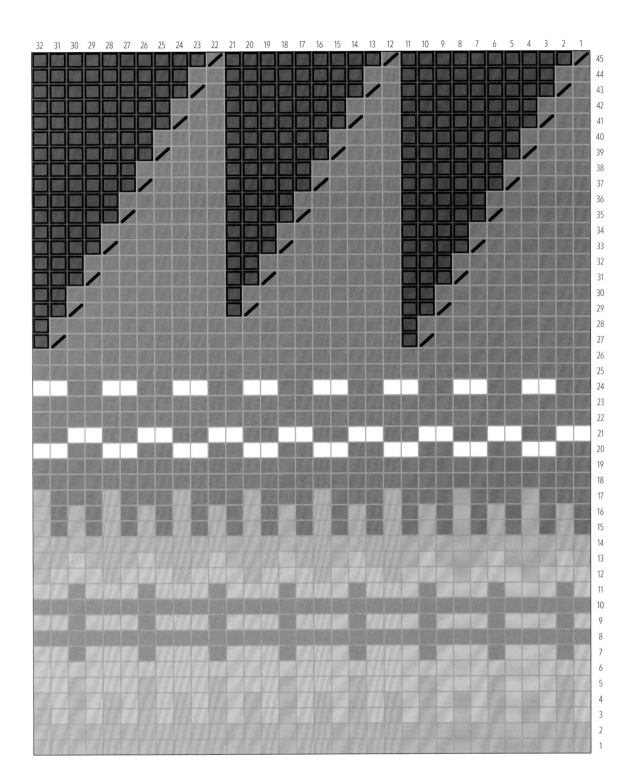

Isle Royale

MICHIGAN

Isle Royale is one of the most remote and least visited of all the national parks. This rugged yet beautiful island rising out of Lake Superior near the Canadian border can only be accessed by ferry, seaplane, or private boat and only during a few months of the year. Once on shore, visitors are immersed in a land of wolves and moose—the only known place where these two species exist without the presence of bears. You could spend three or four days on the island and never see either animal, but the tracks along trails and shorelines serve as a constant reminder of their presence. Using three colors inspired by the subdued hues of a foggy day, this design features bands of the tracks left behind by the elusive moose and wolves. Can you identify which is which?

SIZE

One size fits an average adult
size head (approx. 19 in. /
48 cm to 22 in. / 56 cm).

YARN

A: Malabrigo Rios, Yerba
(25 g / 50 yd. / 46 m)

B: Malabrigo Rios, Fog
(50 g / 100 yd. / 91 m)

C: Peekaboo Yarns Merino
Worsted, Warm Brown
(25 g / 50 yd. / 46 m)

Or other worsted weight
(#4) yarn in three colors.

NEEDLES

- US size 5 / 3.75 mm,
  16 in. long circular
  knitting needles
- US size 7 / 4.5 mm,
  16 in. long circular
  knitting needles
- US size 7 / 4.5 mm double
  pointed needles (DPNs)

Or sizes needed to obtain
gauge.

NOTIONS

- Three stitch markers
  (two of one color and
  one of another color)
- Tapestry needle for
  weaving in ends

GAUGE

With larger needles,
approximately 9½
stitches = 2 in. in
stockinette stitch,
blocked.

With color A and smaller circular needles, cast on 96 stitches. Place single color marker and join in the round being careful not to twist stitches. Work k1, p1 rib pattern for approximately 1½ to 2 in.

Increase row: *k15, knit in front and back of next stitch. Repeat from * to end of round—102 sts total.

Switch to larger needles and work chart from right to left beginning on Row 1, bottom right corner. Chart repeats three times around the hat. Use the two remaining stitch markers of another color to mark chart repeats.

Note: In order to avoid long "floats" (strands of yarn on the inside of the hat) do not carry a color more than three to four stitches without twisting the colors around each other in the back of work.

Switch to DPNs when work becomes too small for circular needles.

FINISHING

After Row 46 is complete, cut yarn leaving a 10 in. tail. Using a tapestry needle, weave tail through remaining stitches and pull tightly to close circle. Pull the tail to the inside and weave in all ends.

Block as desired. See page 12 for wet blocking technique.

Go on adventures!

KEY

▨	A
☐	B
▨	C
☐	Knit k
╱	Knit 2 Together k2tog
▉	No Stitch

Note: The "no stitch" squares represent the stitches that were lost due to decreases earlier in the project. Do not skip a stitch. Simply treat the squares as if they do not exist.

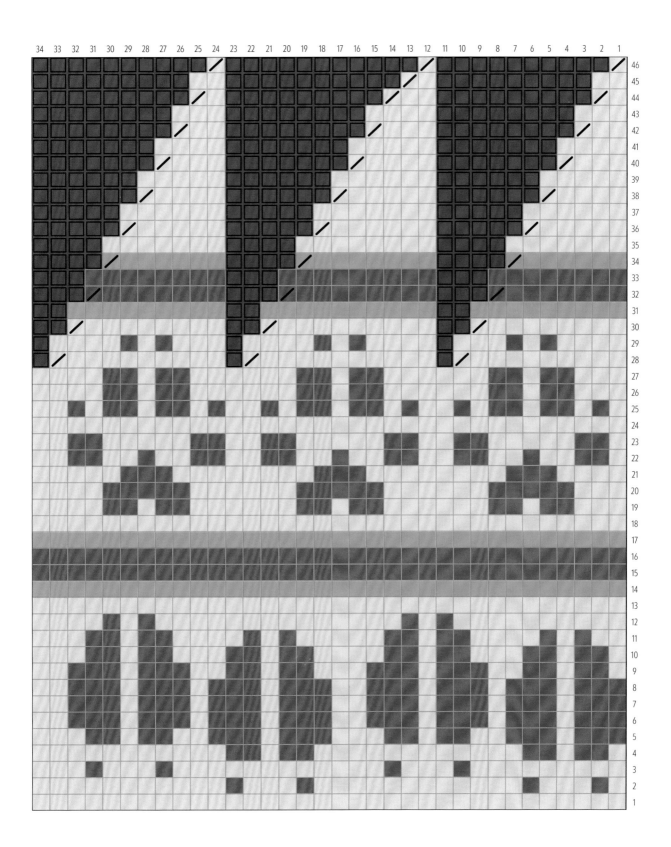

Theodore Roosevelt

NORTH DAKOTA

This sprawling park in North Dakota features three geographically separate areas linked together by the Little Missouri River. Using carefully chosen colors and fun-to-knit images, this design takes you from the bison herds of the grasslands to the red-striped pillars, caprocks, and buttes of the badlands.

SIZE

One size fits an average adult size head (approx. 19 in. / 48 cm to 22 in. / 56 cm).

YARN

Stunning String Legacy Worsted:

- **A:** Black Forest (25 g / 50 yd. / 46 m)
- **B:** Bohemia (20 g / 40 yd. / 37 m)
- **C:** Biscotti (20 g / 40 yd. / 37 m)
- **D:** Coffee Beans (20 g / 40 yd. / 37 m)
- **E:** Roof Tile (20 g / 40 yd. / 37 m)

Or other worsted weight (#4) yarn in five colors.

NEEDLES

- US size 5 / 3.75 mm, 16 in. long circular knitting needles
- US size 7 / 4.5 mm, 16 in. long circular knitting needles
- US size 7 / 4.5 mm double pointed needles (DPNs)

Or sizes needed to obtain gauge.

Continued on next page

NOTIONS

- Four stitch markers (three of one color and one of another color)
- Tapestry needle for weaving in ends

GAUGE

With larger needles, approximately 9½ stitches = 2 in. in stockinette stitch, blocked.

FINISHING

After Row 46 is complete, cut yarn leaving a 10 in. tail. Using a tapestry needle, weave tail through remaining stitches and pull tightly to close circle. Pull the tail to the inside and weave in all ends.

Block as desired. See page 12 for wet blocking technique.

Go on adventures!

KEY

▨	A
▨	B
▨	C
▨	D
▨	E
☐	Knit k
◩	Knit 2 Together k2tog
▨	No Stitch

Note: The "no stitch" squares represent the stitches that were lost due to decreases earlier in the project. Do not skip a stitch. Simply treat the squares as if they do not exist.

With color A and smaller circular needles, cast on 96 stitches. Place single color marker and join in the round being careful not to twist stitches.

Work k1, p1 rib pattern for approximately 1½ to 2 in.

Switch to larger needles and work chart from right to left beginning on Row 1, bottom right corner. Chart will repeat 4 times around the hat. Use the three remaining stitch markers of another color to mark chart repeats.

Note: To avoid long "floats" (strands of yarn on the inside of the hat) do not carry a color more than three to four stitches without twisting the colors around each other in the back of work.

Switch to DPNs when work becomes too small for circular needles.

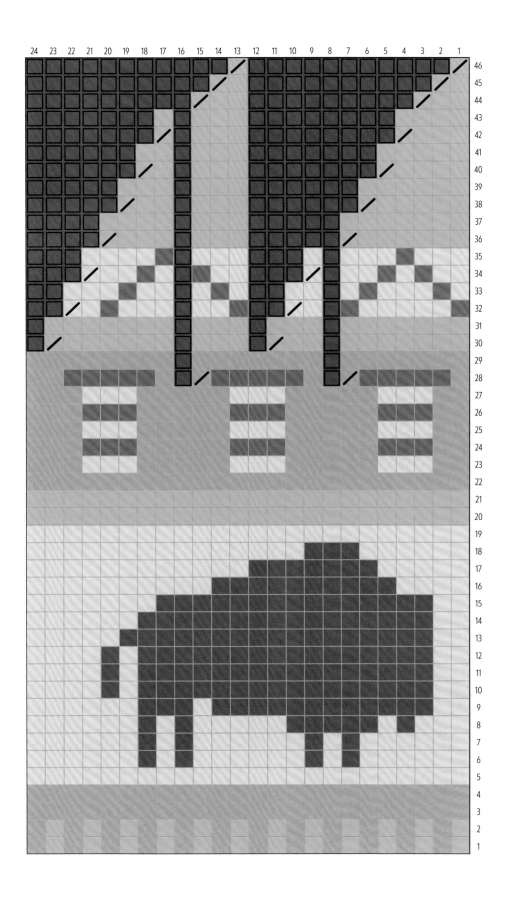

Voyageurs

MINNESOTA

Named after the early French Canadian fur traders, this remote park on the border of the United States and Canada in Minnesota encompasses 30 lakes and over 900 islands. The contrast between islands and water is so stunning that when viewed from the air, the park resembles huge green puzzle pieces scattered across a giant blue mirror. With a maze of waterways to explore, campsites and trails that are only accessible by boat, and a chance of viewing the northern lights, Voyageurs National Park attracts visitors seeking both solitude and adventure. Using carefully placed patches of seed stitch against a background of simple stockinette, this design recreates the beautiful island landscape. You won't end up with 900 islands, but you will have 27!

SIZE

One size fits an average adult size head (approx. 19 in. / 48 cm to 22 in. / 56 cm).

YARN

Peekaboo Yarns Merino Worsted:

A: Zion Blue (50 g / 100 yd. / 91 m)

B: Voyageurs Green (50 g / 100 yd. / 91 m)

Or other worsted weight yarn (#4) in two colors.

NEEDLES

- US size 5 / 3.75 mm, 16 in. long circular knitting needles
- US size 7 / 4.5 mm, 16 in. long circular knitting needles
- US size 7 / 4.5 mm double pointed needles (DPNs)

Or sizes needed to obtain gauge.

NOTIONS

- Three stitch markers (two of one color and one of another color)
- Tapestry needle for weaving in ends

GAUGE

With larger needles, approximately 9½ stitches = 2 in. in stockinette stitch, blocked.

With color A and smaller circular needles, cast on 96 stitches. Place single color marker and join in the round being careful not to twist stitches. Work in k1, p1 rib pattern for approximately 1½ to 2 in.

Switch to larger needles and work chart from right to left beginning on Row 1, bottom right corner. Chart will repeat three times around the hat. Use the two remaining stitch markers of another color to mark chart repeats.

Important Note: In order to avoid long "floats" (strands of yarn on the inside of the hat) do not carry a color more than three to four stitches without twisting the colors around each other in the back of work. Do NOT pull your floats too tightly or your hat will be too small. Be sure to spread out your stitches on your right needle every five stitches or so to help avoid pulling too tightly.

Switch to DPNs when work becomes too small for circular needles.

FINISHING

After Row 44 is complete, cut yarn leaving a 10 in. tail. Using a tapestry needle, weave tail through remaining stitches and pull tightly to close circle. Pull the tail to the inside and weave in all ends.

Block as desired. See page 12 for wet blocking technique.

Go on adventures!

KEY

■	A
■	B
□	Knit k
◪	Knit 2 Together k2tog
⊟	Purl p
◪	Purl 2 Together p2tog
■	No Stitch

Note: The "no stitch" squares represent the stitches that were lost due to decreases earlier in the project. Do not skip a stitch. Simply treat the squares as if they do not exist.

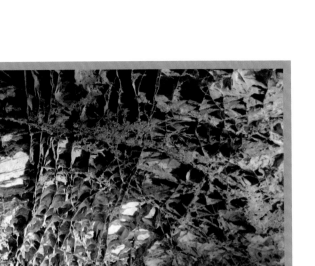

Wind Cave

SOUTH DAKOTA

This biodiverse park in South Dakota is famously home to bison, prairie dogs, and elk, but also filled to the brim with other creatures among its forests, grasslands, and prairies. *Beneath* all this beauty, however, lies one of the longest and most complex caves in the world: Wind Cave. Its name comes from the wind that blows from a small natural entrance to the cave, but its most famous feature is boxwork—the intricate and rare calcite formations found throughout the cave. Using only two colors and an easy to follow chart, this design recreates the perfectly imperfect pattern in a fun hat that would look great in any colors.

SIZE

One size fits an average adult size head (approx. 19 in. / 48 cm to 22 in. / 56 cm).

YARN

Stunning String Legacy Worsted:

■ **A:** Valley Sunset (50 g / 100 yd. / 91 m)

■ **B:** Pine Cone (50 g / 100 yd. / 91 m)

Or other worsted weight (#4) yarn in two colors.

NEEDLES

- US size 5 / 3.75 mm, 16 in. long circular knitting needles
- US size 7 / 4.5 mm, 16 in. long circular knitting needles
- US size 7 / 4.5 mm double pointed needles (DPNs)

Or sizes needed to obtain gauge.

NOTIONS

- Four stitch markers (three of one color and one of another color)
- Tapestry needle for weaving in ends

GAUGE

With larger needles, approximately 9½ stitches = 2 in. in stockinette stitch, blocked.

With smaller circular needles and color A, cast on 96 stitches. Place single color marker and join in the round being careful not to twist stitches. Work k1, p1 rib pattern for approximately 1½ to 2 in.

Increase row: *k23, knit in front and back of next stitch. Repeat from * to end of round—100 sts total.

Switch to larger needles and work chart from right to left beginning on Row 1, bottom right corner. Chart repeats four times around the hat. Use the three remaining stitch markers of another color to mark chart repeats.

Note: To avoid long "floats" (strands of yarn on the inside of the hat) do not carry a color more than three to four stitches without twisting the colors around each other in the back of work.

Switch to DPNs when work becomes too small for circular needles.

FINISHING

After Row 44 is complete, cut yarn leaving a 10 in. tail. Using a tapestry needle, weave tail through remaining stitches and pull tightly to close circle. Pull the tail to the inside and weave in all ends.

Block as desired. See page 12 for wet blocking technique.

Go on adventures!

KEY

 A

 B

☐ Knit
k

◨ Knit 2 Together
k2tog

■ No Stitch

Note: The "no stitch" squares represent the stitches that were lost due to decreases earlier in the project. Do not skip a stitch. Simply treat the squares as if they do not exist.

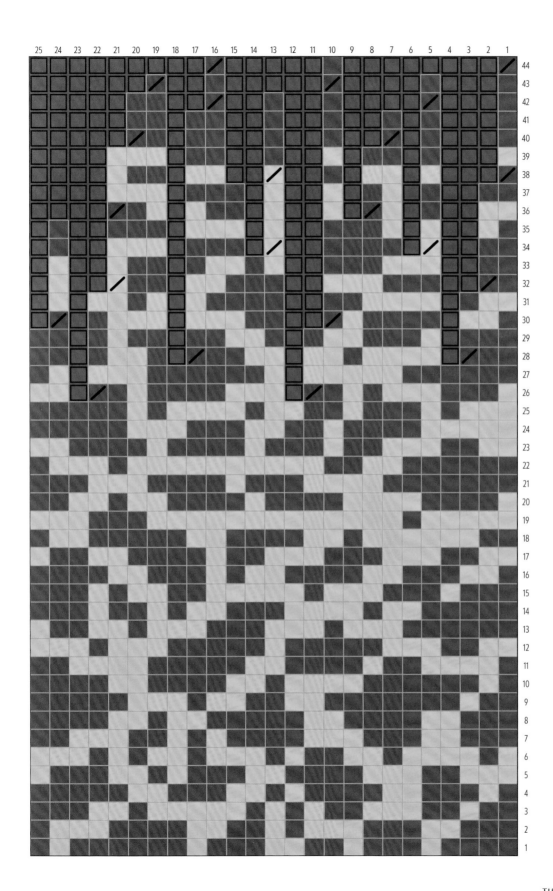

Arches

UTAH

Sixty-five million years of incredible geologic forces and the power of erosion have sculpted a landscape in Utah that seems impossible. Over 2,000 stone arches spanning distances of up to 300 feet stand among pillars, fins, pinnacles, and balancing rocks. The contrast of bright green trees and shrubs against red-orange rock and blue skies has entranced hikers and campers for generations, bringing a feeling of awe and wonder not easily forgotten. Featuring a color as warm as the sunsets that grace the landscape, this beanie uses cable stitches to create a double arch embossed against a subtly textured backdrop of rows of knits and purls. Blue sky peeks through arches in the distance.

SIZE

One size fits an average adult size head (approx. 19 in. / 48 cm to 22 in. / 56 cm).

YARN

Aly Bee Workshop Merino Worsted:

A: Peaches (75 g / 150 yd. / 137 m)

B: Glass Slipper (20 g / 40 yd. / 37 m)

Or other worsted weight yarn (#4) in two colors.

NEEDLES

- US size 5 / 3.75 mm, 16 in. long circular knitting needles
- US size 7 / 4.5 mm, 16 in. long circular knitting needles
- US size 7 / 4.5 mm double pointed needles (DPNs)

Or sizes needed to obtain gauge.

NOTIONS

- Three stitch markers (two of one color and one of another color)
- Tapestry needle for weaving in ends
- Cable needle (cn)

GAUGE

With larger needles, approximately 9½ stitches = 2 in. in stockinette stitch, blocked.

With color A and smaller circular needles, cast on 96 stitches. Place single color marker and join in the round being careful not to twist stitches. Work in k1, p1 rib pattern for approximately 1½ in.

Increase row: *k15, knit in front and back of next stitch. Repeat from * to end of round. 6 increases made—102 sts total.

Switch to larger needles and work chart from right to left beginning on Row 1, bottom right corner. Chart repeats three times around the hat. Use the two remaining stitch markers of another color to mark chart repeats.

Note: In order to avoid long "floats" (strands of yarn on the inside of the hat) do not carry a color more than three to four stitches without twisting the colors around each other in the back of work.

Switch to DPNs when work becomes too small for circular needles.

FINISHING

After Row 46 is complete, cut yarn leaving a 10 in. tail. Using a tapestry needle, weave tail through remaining stitches and pull tightly to close circle. Pull the tail to the inside and weave in all ends.

Block as desired. See page 12 for wet blocking technique.

Go on adventures!

KEY

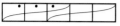

▨ A

▨ B

■ No Stitch

Note: The "no stitch" squares represent the stitches that were lost due to decreases earlier in the project. Do not skip a stitch. Simply treat these squares as if they do not exist.

☐ Knit
k

⊟ Purl
p

◹ Knit 2 Together
k2tog

◺ Slip 3 Together Purlwise, Knit 2 Together, Pass 3 Slipped Stitches over
s3tog-k2tog-p3sso

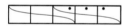

4/1 Right Purl Cable
4/1 rpc
Slip 1 to cn, hold in back, k4, p1 from cn

2/3 Left Purl Cable
2/3 lpc
Slip 2 to cn, hold in front, p3, k2 from cn

2/3 Right Purl Cable
2/3 rpc
Slip 3 to cn, hold in back, k2, p3 from cn

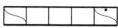

4/1 Left Purl Cable
4/1 lpc
Slip 4 to cn, hold in front, p1, k4 from cn

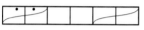

4/2 Right Purl Cable
4/2 rpc
Slip 2 to cn, hold in back, k4, p2 from cn

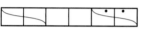

4/2 Left Purl Cable
4/2 lpc
Slip 4 to cn, hold in front, p2, k4 from cn

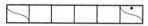

5/1 Left Purl Cable
5/1 lpc
Slip 5 to cn, hold in front, p1, k5 from cn

Helpful hint: This design features several different right and left leaning purl crossover/cable stitches. Count carefully and pay close attention to make sure you are working the correct stitch. Leaning your stitch the wrong way will drastically alter the shape of the arches.

Big Bend

TEXAS

There's a place in west Texas where the desert meets the mountains, rivers carve majestic canyons, night skies sparkle with millions of stars, and—in early spring after the rain—bluebonnets line the roadsides and turn the hillsides blue. This is Big Bend! Inspired by a springtime bloom on a sunny day, this beanie features rich colors from the desert floor and bluebonnet fields to the browns and golds of the subtly textured mountains. Simple embroidery stitches add dimension and even more color to the beloved state flower of Texas.

SIZE

One size fits an average adult size head (approx. 19 in. / 48 cm to 22 in. / 56 cm).

YARN

A: Stunning String Studio Legacy Worsted, Desert Floor (Color used for ribbing; not shown on chart) (25 g / 50 yd. / 46 m)

☐ **B:** Stunning String Studio Legacy Worsted, Desert Bloom (25 g / 50 yd. / 46 m)

☐ **C:** Aly Bee Workshop Superwash Merino Worsted, Bluebonnets (25 g / 50 yd. / 46 m)

☐ **D:** Stunning String Studio Legacy Worsted, Valley Sunset (25 g / 50 yd. / 46 m)

A few yards of light yellow (Aly Bee Workshop Superwash Merino Worsted, Lemon-Lime) for embroidering tops of the bluebonnets.

Or other worsted weight yarn (#4) in five colors.

NEEDLES

- US size 5 / 3.75 mm, 16 in. long circular knitting needles
- US size 7 / 4.5 mm, 16 in. long circular knitting needles
- US size 7 / 4.5 mm double pointed needles (DPNs)

Or sizes needed to obtain gauge.

Continued on next page

NOTIONS

- Three stitch markers (two of one color and one of another color)
- Tapestry needle for weaving in ends and embroidering flowers

GAUGE

With larger needles, approximately 9½ stitches = 2 in. in stockinette stitch, blocked.

Note: If you already know you are a tight knitter, go up one needle size for both the ribbing and the body of the hat.

With color A and smaller circular needles, cast on 96 stitches. Place single color marker and join in the round being careful not to twist stitches. Work in k1, p1 rib pattern for approximately 1½ in.

Increase row: *k10, kfb, k9, kfb, k10, kfb. Repeat from * to end of round—105 sts (Note: kfb = knit in front and back)

Switch to larger needles and work chart from right to left beginning on Row 1, bottom right corner. Chart repeats three times around the hat. Use the two remaining stitch markers of another color to mark chart repeats.

Note: In order to avoid long "floats" (strands of yarn on the inside of the hat) do not carry a color more than three to four stitches without twisting the colors around each other in the back of work.

Switch to DPNs when work becomes too small for circular needles.

FINISHING

After Row 45 is complete, cut yarn leaving a 10 in. tail. Using a tapestry needle, weave tail through remaining stitches and pull tightly to close circle. Pull the tail to the inside and weave in all ends.

Block hat to smooth and even out stitches. See page 12 for wet blocking technique.

Once your hat is finished and blocked, add embroidery stitches to take the bluebonnets from simple lines to dimensional plants. These stitches will bring the hat to life!

1. Thread tapestry needle with about 20 inches of color C. Longer lengths tend to tangle.

2. After anchoring your yarn on the inside of the hat by weaving back and forth for an inch or so, bring the yarn up the middle of one of the taller stems. Start at about 3 to 6 stitches from the bottom of the stem.

3. Bring needle down through hat about 2 to 3 stitches to the right and up from starting point. Pull yarn through, creating your first stitch.

4.

Bring needle up though the middle of stem again and repeat, to the left this time.

5. Continue moving up the stem creating various sizes and angles of stitches.

6.

Once you've reached the top of the stem, begin working your way down adding single and double wrap French knots as desired.

7.

When all the bluebonnets have been embroidered, go back and add 2 or 3 stitches of the light-yellow yarn to the tops of some of the plants.

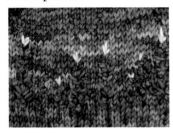

IMPORTANT NOTES ABOUT EMBROIDERING YOUR FLOWERS

- Your flowers will look more organic/natural if they are not perfectly symmetrical. Be sure to vary the length and angle of your stitches.

- Not every stem needs to be embroidered the same amount, or even at all. Some blue areas are meant to be background. Up-close flowers get more detail.

- Weave in your ends every time you start and finish a new strand of embroidery yarn.

- Enjoy the process. Yes, it takes time (it took me 2½ hours!) ... but you are creating wearable art! Every hat is unique and different.

Go on adventures!

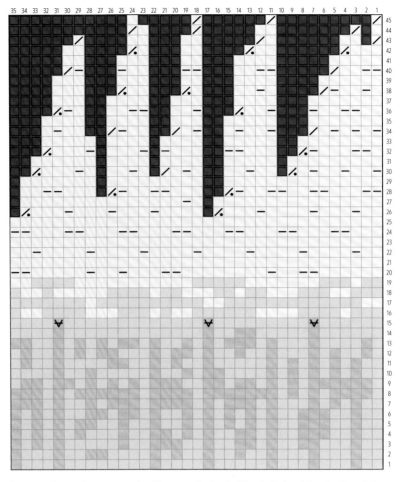

Row 15: No need to carry color C across the back. Simply knit with color B and then slip color C where shown.

KEY

▢	B
▨	C
▢	D
▢	Knit k
◢	Knit 2 Together k2tog

⊟	Purl p
◢•	Purl 2 Together p2tog
⋁	Slip Purlwise with Yarn in Back slwyib
■	No Stitch

Note: The "no stitch" squares represent the stitches that were lost due to decreases earlier in the project. Do not skip a stitch. Simply treat the squares as if they do not exist.

Black Canyon
of the Gunnison

COLORADO

This beautiful gem in Colorado may be one of the lesser-known national parks, but it contains some of the deepest, steepest, and most spectacular canyons and cliffs in the country. A perfect example of "art created by nature," the famous Painted Wall—with its dark gray Precambrian cliffs striped with pink bands of pegmatite—stands nearly 1,000 feet taller than the Empire State Building. This beanie features nature-inspired semi-solid colors with just a hint of sparkle to represent the mica found in the pink layers.

SIZE

One size fits an average adult size head (approx. 19 in. / 48 cm to 22 in. / 56 cm).

YARN

A: Anzula Cricket DK, Charcoal (60 g /125 yd. / 113 m)

B: Anzula Lucero DK, Mauve (40 g / 90 yd. / 82 m)

Or other DK weight yarn (#3) in two colors.

NEEDLES

- US size 4 / 3.5 mm, 16 in. long circular knitting needles
- US size 6 / 4 mm, 16 in. long circular knitting needles
- US size 6 / 4 mm double pointed needles (DPNs)

Or sizes needed to obtain gauge.

NOTIONS

- Two stitch markers in different colors
- Tapestry needle for weaving in ends

GAUGE

With larger needles, approximately 11 stitches = 2 in. in stockinette stitch, blocked.

With color A and smaller circular needles, cast on 104 stitches. Place single color marker and join in the round being careful not to twist stitches. Work in k1, p1 rib pattern for approximately 1½ to 2 in.

Increase row: *k25, kfb in next stitch. Repeat from * around. 4 increases made—108 sts.

Switch to larger needles and work chart from right to left beginning on Row 1, bottom right corner. Chart repeats twice around the hat. Use remaining stitch marker of another color to mark chart repeat.

Note: In order to avoid long "floats" (strands of yarn on the inside of the hat) do not carry a color more than three to four stitches without twisting the colors around each other in the back of work. Do NOT pull your floats too tightly or your hat will be too small. Be sure to spread out your stitches on your right needle every five stitches or so to help avoid pulling too tightly.

Switch to DPNs when work becomes too small for circular needles.

FINISHING:

After Row 46 is complete, cut yarn leaving a 10 in. tail. Using a tapestry needle, weave tail through remaining stitches and pull tightly to close circle. Pull the tail to the inside and weave in all ends.

Block as desired. See page 12 for wet blocking technique.

Go on adventures!

KEY

▧	A
▨	B
☐	Knit k
◪	Knit 2 Together k2tog
◼	No Stitch

Note: The "no stitch" squares represent the stitches that were lost due to decreases earlier in the project. Do not skip a stitch. Simply treat the squares as if they do not exist.

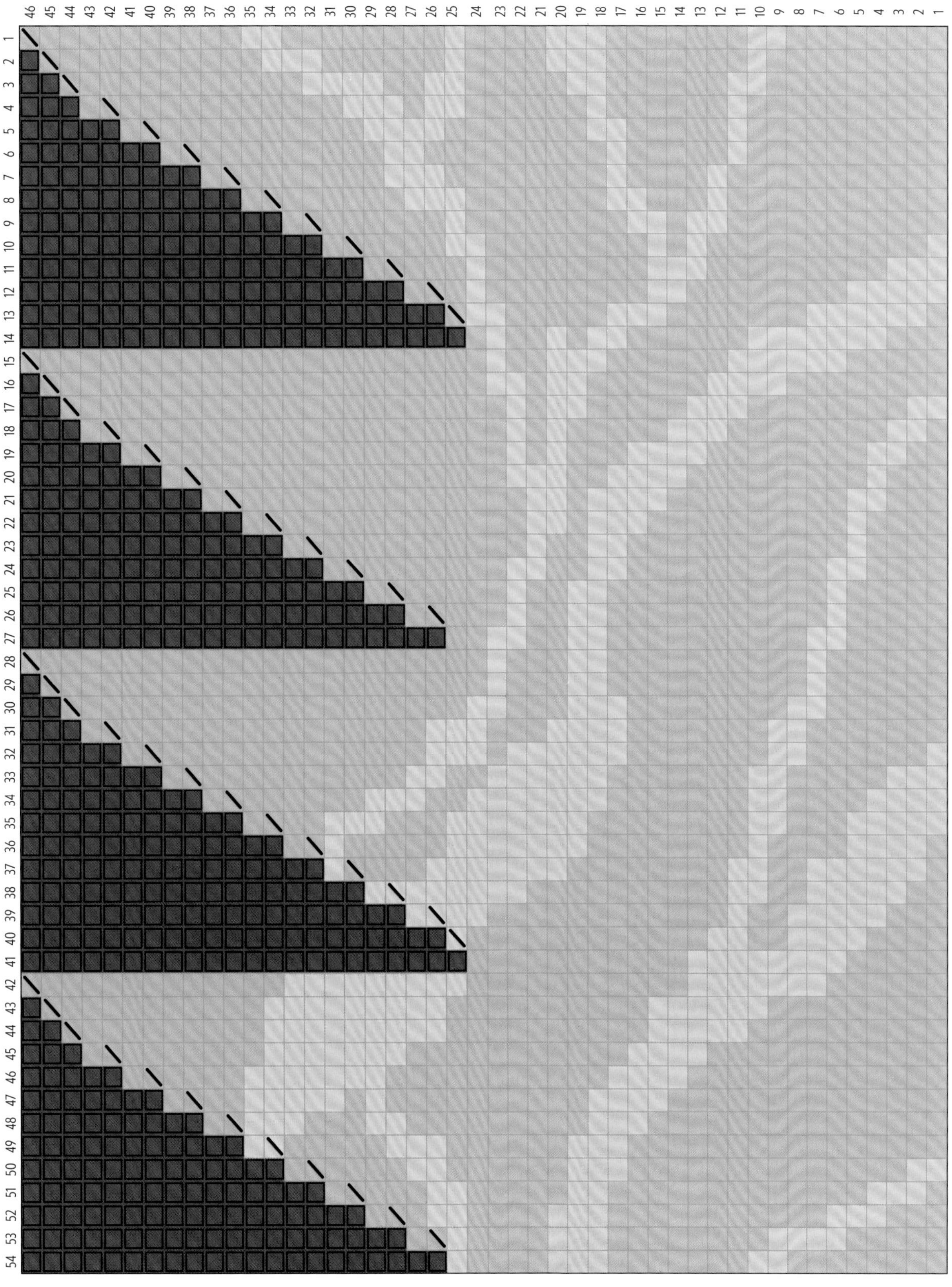

Bryce Canyon

UTAH

Bryce Canyon is home to the world's largest collection of hoodoos, the oddly shaped and beautiful stone columns created by thousands of years of erosion. These tall spires in layers of oranges, reds, and pinks are so plentiful that it's easy to see why the canyon is sometimes called "A Forest of Stone." This beanie features layers of warm orange tones and subtle texture with understated vertical stitches creating offset columns that narrow toward the top of the hat, much like the hoodoos themselves.

SIZE

One size fits an average adult size head (approx. 19 in. / 48 cm to 22 in. / 56 cm).

YARN

- **A:** Malabrigo Rios, Sunset (50 g / 100 yd. / 91 m)
- **B:** Peekaboo Yarns Superwash Merino Worsted, Orange Blaze (20 g / 40 yd. / 37 m)
- **C:** Stunning String Legacy Worsted, Fading Sunlight (13 g / 25 yd. / 23 m)
- **D:** Cascade 220 Superwash Effects, Lava (20 g / 40 yd. / 37 m)

Or other worsted weight (#4) yarn in four colors.

NEEDLES

- US size 5 / 3.75 mm, 16 in. long circular knitting needles
- US size 7 / 4.5 mm, 16 in. long circular knitting needles
- US size 7 / 4.5 mm double pointed needles (DPNs)

Or sizes needed to obtain gauge.

Continued on next page

NOTIONS

- Three stitch markers (two of one color and one of another color)
- Tapestry needle for weaving in ends

GAUGE

With larger needles, approximately 9 stitches = 2 in. in stockinette stitch.

With color A and smaller circular needles, cast on 96 stitches. Place single color marker and join in the round being careful not to twist stitches.

Work rib pattern for approximately 1½ to 2 in.

Rib pattern: *k1 tbl, (p1, k1) 3 times, p1. Repeat from * to end of round.

Switch to larger needles and work chart from right to left beginning on Row 1, bottom right corner. Chart repeats three times around the hat. Use the two remaining stitch markers of another color to mark chart repeats.

Switch to DPNs when work becomes too small for circular needles.

FINISHING

After Row 47 is complete, cut yarn leaving a 10 in. tail. Using a tapestry needle, weave tail through remaining stitches and pull tightly to close circle. Pull the tail to the inside and weave in all ends.

Block as desired. See page 12 for wet blocking technique.

Go on adventures!

KEY

▨	A
▨	B
☐	C
■	D
☐	Knit k
⧄	Knit 1 Through Back Loop k1 tbl
╱	Knit 2 Together k2tog
⊟	Purl p
╱	Purl 2 Together p2tog
■	No Stitch

Note: The "no stitch" squares represent the stitches that were lost due to decreases earlier in the project. Do not skip a stitch. Simply treat the squares as if they do not exist.

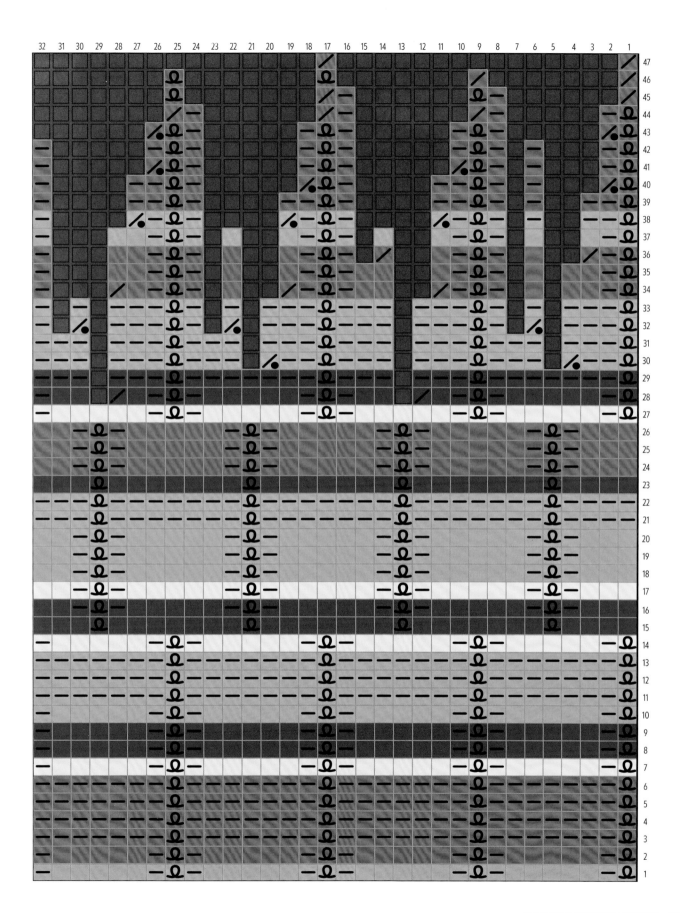

Canyonlands

UTAH

T he Green and Colorado Rivers have been carving out canyons in the high desert of southeast Utah for millions of years. The forces of erosion and the wonders of geologic movement continue to shape the mesas, buttes, spires, and arches of the Canyonlands we see today. The resulting landscape is the ideal location for adventures of all types or for a simple drive along the paved park road with its many overlooks. Using rich colors and simple stitches, you can recreate one of these amazing overlook views from the vertical texture of the canyon walls to the smooth mesa tops.

SIZE

One size fits an average adult size head (approx. 19 in. / 48 cm to 22 in. / 56 cm).

YARN

■ **A:** Malabrigo Rios, Volcan (50 g / 100 yd. / 91 m)

■ **B:** Peekaboo Yarns Merino Worsted, Wheat Fields (50 g / 100 yd. / 91 m)

Or other worsted weight (#4) yarn in two colors.

NEEDLES

- US size 5 / 3.75 mm, 16 in. long circular knitting needles
- US size 7 / 4.5 mm, 16 in. long circular knitting needles
- US size 7 / 4.5 mm double pointed needles (DPNs)

Or sizes needed to obtain gauge.

NOTIONS

- Three stitch markers (two of one color and one of another color)
- Tapestry needle for weaving in ends

GAUGE

With larger needles, approximately 9½ stitches = 2 in. in stranded stockinette stitch.

Note: If you already know you are a tight knitter, go up one needle size for both the ribbing and the body of the hat.

With color A and smaller circular needles, cast on 96 stitches. Place single color marker and join in the round being careful not to twist stitches. Work p1, k1 tbl (through back loop) rib pattern for approximately 1½ to 2 in.

Switch to larger needles and work chart from right to left beginning on Row 1, bottom right corner. Chart repeats three times around the hat. Use the two remaining stitch markers of another color to mark chart repeats.

Note: In order to avoid long "floats" (strands of yarn on the inside of the hat) do not carry a color more than three to four stitches without twisting the colors around each other in the back of work.

Note: Catching floats behind a knit stitch (rather than a purl) will have less chance of "show through" on the right side.

Switch to DPNs when work becomes too small for circular needles.

FINISHING

After Row 46 is complete, cut yarn leaving a 10 in. tail. Using a tapestry needle, weave tail through remaining stitches and pull tightly to close circle. Pull the tail to the inside and weave in all ends.

Block as desired. See page 12 for wet blocking technique.

Go on adventures!

KEY

■	A
■	B
□	Knit k
⧀	Knit 1 Through Back Loop k1 tbl
⧄	Knit 2 Together k2tog
⧅	Knit 2 Together Through the Back Loop k2tog tbl
▭	Purl p
■	No Stitch

Note: The "no stitch" squares represent the stitches that were lost due to decreases earlier in the project. Do not skip a stitch. Simply treat the squares as if they do not exist.

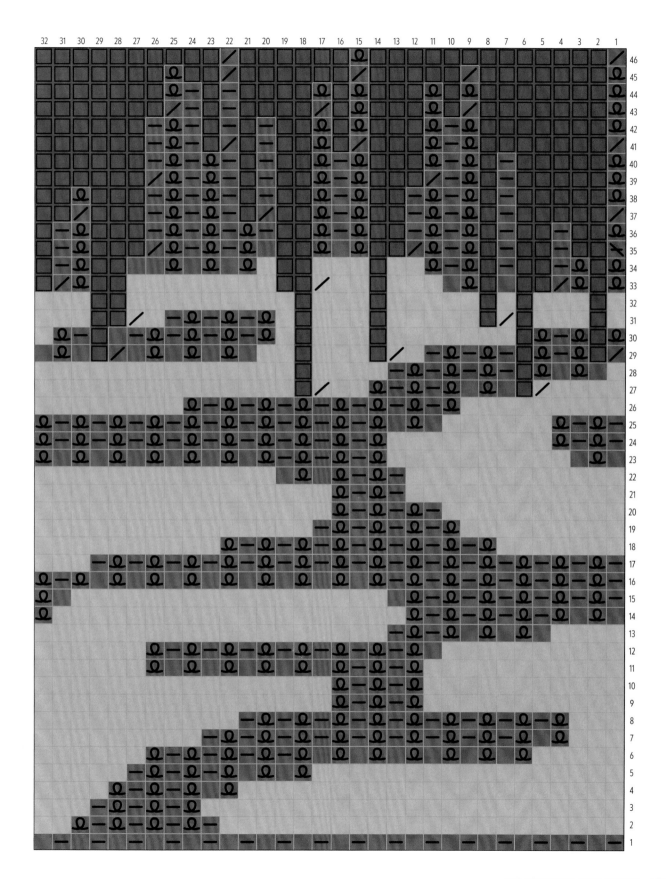

Capitol Reef

UTAH

Capitol Reef National Park is a delightful and unexpected mix of pioneer homesteads, historic orchards, scenic drives, yummy homemade pies, and nearly 200 million years of spectacular geologic history. Rows of textured stitches and carefully chosen colors recreate the beautiful rock layers, including the characteristic gray-green of the smooth Chinle Formation.

SIZE

One size fits an average adult size head (approx. 19 in. / 48 cm to 22 in. / 56 cm).

YARN

A: Peekaboo Yarns Merino Worsted, Burnt Orange (25 g / 50 yd. / 46 m)

B: Peekaboo Yarns Merino Worsted, Moonstone (17 g / 35 yd. / 32 m)

C: Peekaboo Yarns Merino Worsted, Red Rock West (17 g / 35 yd. / 32 m)

D: Peekaboo Yarns Merino Worsted, Wheat Fields (17 g / 35 yd. / 32 m)

E: Malabrigo Rios, Camel (20 g / 40 yd. / 37 m)

Or other worsted weight (#4) yarn in five colors.

NEEDLES

- US size 5 / 3.75 mm, 16 in. long circular knitting needles
- US size 7 / 4.5 mm, 16 in. long circular knitting needles
- US size 7 / 4.5 mm double pointed needles (DPNs)

Or sizes needed to obtain gauge.

Continued on next page

NOTIONS

- Four stitch markers (three of one color and one of another color)
- Tapestry needle for weaving in ends

GAUGE

With larger needles, approximately 9½ stitches = 2 in. in stockinette stitch, blocked.

With color A and smaller circular needles, cast on 96 stitches. Place single color marker and join in the round being careful not to twist stitches. Work k1, p1 rib pattern for approximately 1½ to 2 in.

Switch to larger needles and work chart from right to left beginning on Row 1, bottom right corner. Chart repeats four times around the hat. Use the three remaining stitch markers of another color to mark chart repeats.

Switch to DPNs when work becomes too small for circular needles.

FINISHING

After Row 47 is complete, cut yarn leaving a 10 in. tail. Using a tapestry needle, weave tail through remaining stitches and pull tightly to close circle. Pull the tail to the inside and weave in all ends.

Block as desired. See page 12 for wet blocking technique.

Go on adventures!

KEY

- A
- B
- C
- D
- E

⋁ Increase 1 to 3
Purl, knit, purl in one stitch

Knit
k

╱ Knit 2 Together
k2tog

⋀ Knit 3 Together
k3tog

— Purl
p

⋒ Purl 1 Through Back Loop
p1 tbl

╱. Purl 2 Together
p2tog

No Stitch

Note: The "no stitch" squares represent the stitches that were lost due to decreases earlier in the project. Do not skip a stitch. Simply treat the squares as if they do not exist.

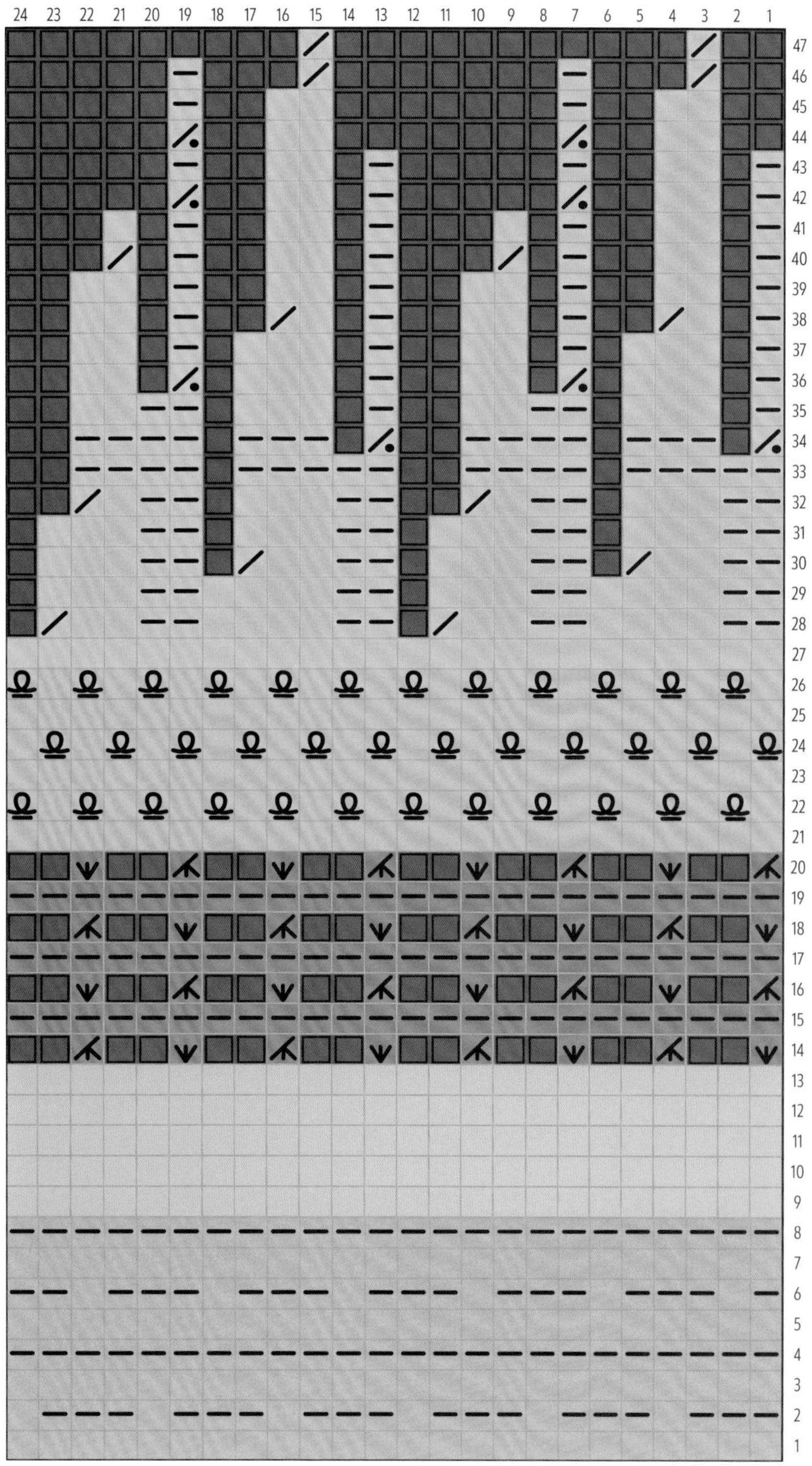

Carlsbad Caverns

NEW MEXICO

Carlsbad Caverns is a huge and complex cave system, with more than 119 caves in total! Drip by drip, over the course of a million years, beautiful and unusual formations built up within the caverns. These formations, with names like soda straws, draperies, ribbons, lily pads, shelves (and of course stalagmites and stalactites), grow on the floor and ceiling and sometimes meet in the middle. Using a variety of fun cables and patterns, your hat will grow its own interesting formations, stitch by stitch. When cave formations meet knitting, fun things are bound to happen.

SIZE

One size fits an average adult size head (approx. 19 in. / 48 cm to 22 in. / 56 cm).

YARN

A: Lion Brand Heartland, Great Sand Dunes (100 g / 200 yd. / 183 m)

Or other worsted weight yarn (#4).

NEEDLES

- US size 5 / 3.75 mm, 16 in. long circular knitting needles
- US size 7 / 4.5 mm, 16 in. long circular knitting needles
- US size 7 / 4.5 mm double pointed needles (DPNs)

Or sizes needed to obtain gauge.

NOTIONS

- Three stitch markers (two of one color and one of another color)
- Tapestry needle for weaving in ends
- Cable needle (cn)

GAUGE

With smaller needles, approx. 11 stitches = 2 in. in 1 × 1 rib pattern, unstretched.

Note: If you already know you are a tight knitter, go up one needle size for both the ribbing and the body of the hat.

With color A and smaller circular needles, cast on 96 stitches. Place single color marker and join in the round being careful not to twist stitches. Work in k1, p1 rib pattern for approximately 1½ in.

Switch to larger needles and work chart from right to left beginning on Row 1, bottom right corner. Chart repeats three times around the hat. Use the two remaining stitch markers of another color to mark chart repeats.

Switch to DPNs when work becomes too small for circular needles.

FINISHING

After Row 46 is complete, cut yarn leaving a 10 in. tail. Using a tapestry needle, weave tail through remaining stitches and pull tightly to close circle. Pull the tail to the inside and weave in all ends.

Block as desired. See page 12 for wet blocking technique.

Go on adventures!

KEY

1/1 Left Purl Cable
Slip 1 to cn, hold in front, p1, k1 from cn

1/1 Right Purl Cable
Slip 1 to cn, hold in back, k1, p1 from cn

1/1 Left Cross
Slip 1 to cn, hold in front, k1, k1 from cn

1/1 Right Cross
Slip 1 to cn, hold in back, k1, k1 from cn

2/1 Left Cross
Slip 2 to cn, hold in front, k1, k2 from cn

2/1 Left Purl Cable
Slip 2 to cn, hold in front, p1, k2 from cn

2/1 Right Cross
Slip 1 to cn, hold in back, k2, k1 from cn

2/1 Right Purl Cable
Slip 1 to cn, hold in back, k2, p1 from cn

Cable 4 Back
Slip 2 to cn, hold in back, k2, k2 from cn

Cable 4 Front
Slip 2 to cn, hold in front, k2, k2 from cn

Cable 6 Back
Slip 3 to cn, hold in back, k3, k3 from cn

Cable 6 Front
Slip 3 to cn, hold in front, k3, k3 from cn

Knit
k

Knit 2 Together
k2tog

Kfsb (knit front, slip back)
Knit stitch without transferring to right needle.
Insert needle in back leg, slip both to right needle.

Purl
p

Purl 2 Together
p2tog

Slip, Slip, Knit Slipped Stitches Together
ssk

No Stitch

Note: The "no stitch" squares represent the stitches that were lost due to decreases earlier in the round. Do not skip a stitch. Simply treat these squares as if they do not exist.

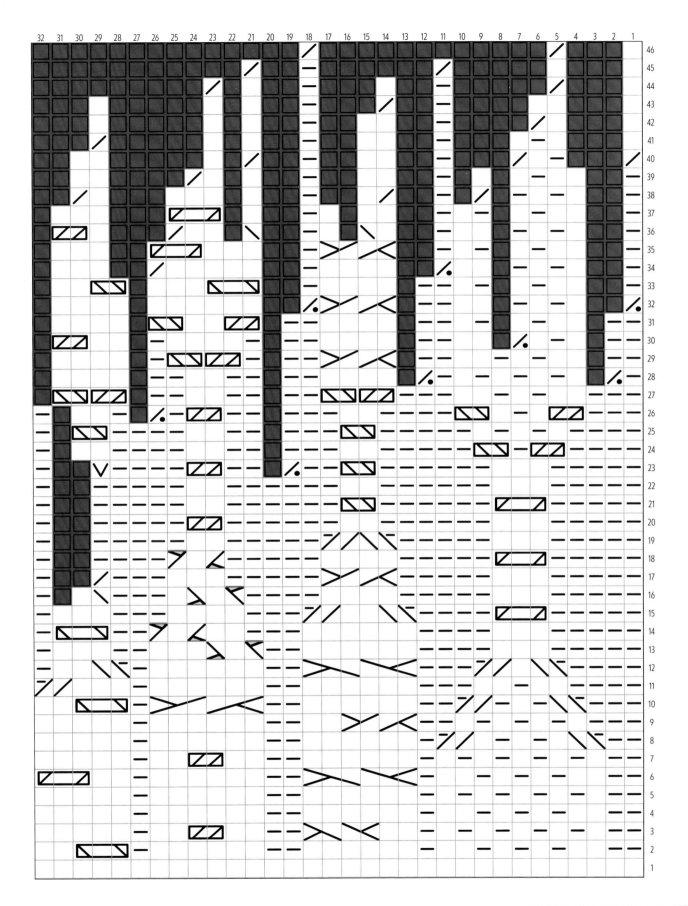

Glacier

MONTANA

Of the 700+ lakes found within the forests and mountains of Glacier National Park, the colorful stones lining the shore of beautiful Lake McDonald make it one of the most photographed. This beanie uses subdued colors and smooth stitches to capture the serenity of the scene from the colorful pebbles on the shore and in shallow water, to the deeper blue of the lake, mountains, and sky—resulting in an overall sense of tranquility.

SIZE

One size fits an average adult size head (approx. 19 in. / 48 cm to 22 in. / 56 cm).

YARN

Western Sky Knits Merino 17 Worsted:

☐ **A:** Bliss (33 g / 36 yd. / 61 m)

☐ **B:** Fallen (17 g / 35 yd. / 32 m)

■ **C:** North Sea (33 g / 66 yd. / 61 m)

☐ **D:** Peppered (17 g / 35 yd. / 32 m)

Or other worsted weight (#4) yarn in four colors.

NEEDLES

- US size 5 / 3.75 mm, 16 in. long circular knitting needles
- US size 7 / 4.5 mm, 16 in. long circular knitting needles
- US size 7 / 4.5 mm double pointed needles (DPNs)

Or sizes needed to obtain gauge.

NOTIONS

- Three stitch markers (two of one color and one of another color)
- Tapestry needle for weaving in ends

GAUGE

With larger needles, approximately 9½ stitches = 2 in. in stockinette stitch.

With color A and smaller circular needles, cast on 96 stitches. Place single color marker and join in the round being careful not to twist stitches.

Work k1, p1 rib pattern for approximately 1½ to 2 in.

Increase row: *k16, M1. Repeat from * around—102 sts total.

Switch to larger needles and work chart from right to left beginning on Row 1, bottom right corner. Chart repeats three times around the hat. Use the two remaining stitch markers of another color to mark chart repeats.

Note: In order to avoid long "floats" (strands of yarn on the inside of the hat) do not carry a color more than three to four stitches without twisting the colors around each other in the back of work.

Switch to DPNs when work becomes too small for circular needles.

FINISHING

After Row 45 is complete, cut yarn leaving a 10 in. tail. Using a tapestry needle, weave tail through remaining stitches and pull tightly to close circle. Pull the tail to the inside and weave in all ends.

Block as desired. See page 12 for wet blocking technique.

Go on adventures!

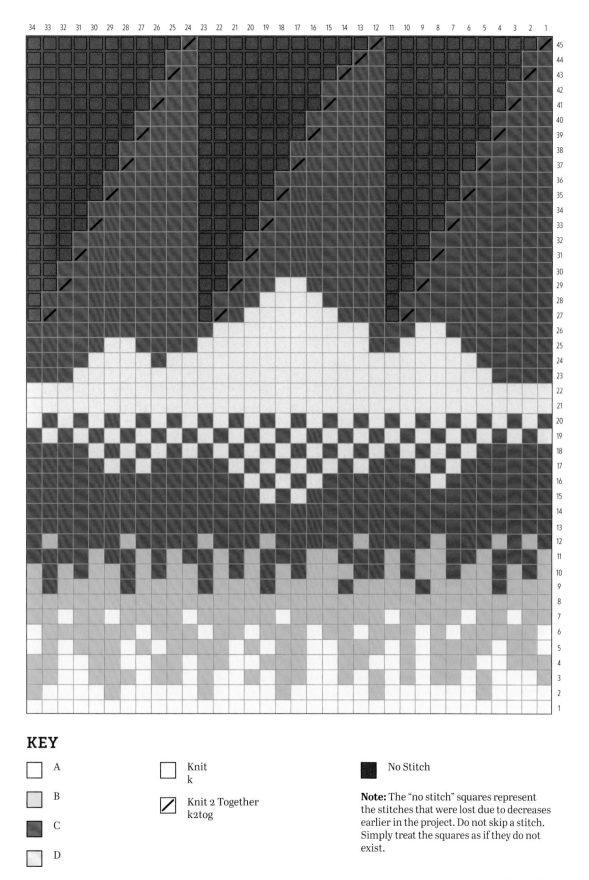

KEY

- ☐ A
- ☐ B
- ■ C
- ☐ D

- ☐ Knit
  k
- ⧄ Knit 2 Together
  k2tog

- ■ No Stitch

Note: The "no stitch" squares represent the stitches that were lost due to decreases earlier in the project. Do not skip a stitch. Simply treat the squares as if they do not exist.

Grand Canyon

ARIZONA

Inspired by the geologic wonder and beauty of the most famous canyon in the world, this beanie takes its cue from the many layers and textures of the canyon walls that change colors as the sun moves across the sky. Using simple combinations of knits and purls, this beanie is easy enough for beginners, yet engaging enough for advanced knitters. Try it in various color combinations for a completely different look.

SIZE

One size fits an average adult size head (approx. 19 in. / 48 cm to 22 in. / 56 cm).

YARN

A: Aly Bee Workshop Merino Worsted, Driftwood (25 g / 50 yd. / 46 m)

B: Peekaboo Yarns Merino Worsted, Yam (33 g / 66 yd. / 60 m)

C: Stunning String Legacy Worsted, Fading Sunlight (17 g / 34 yd. / 31 m)

D: Peekaboo Yarns Merino Worsted, Silverstone (13 g / 25 yd. / 23 m)

E: Aly Bee Workshop Merino Worsted, Kettle Corn (13 g / 25 yd. / 23 m)

Or other worsted weight (#4) yarn in five colors.

NEEDLES

- US size 5 / 3.75 mm, 16 in. long circular knitting needles
- US size 7 / 4.5 mm, 16 in. long circular knitting needles
- US size 7 / 4.5 mm double pointed needles (DPNs)

Or sizes needed to obtain gauge.

Continued on next page

NOTIONS

- Four stitch markers (three of one color and one of another color)
- Tapestry needle for weaving in ends

GAUGE

With larger needles, approximately 9 stitches = 2 in. in stockinette stitch.

With color A and smaller circular needles, cast on 96 stitches. Place single color marker and join in the round being careful not to twist stitches.

Work in k2, p2 rib for approximately 2 in.

Switch to larger needles and work chart from right to left beginning on Row 1, bottom right corner. Chart repeats four times around the hat. Use the three remaining stitch markers of another color to mark chart repeats.

Switch to DPNs when work becomes too small for circular needles.

FINISHING

After Row 47 is complete, cut yarn leaving a 10 in. tail. Using a tapestry needle, weave tail through remaining eight stitches and pull tightly to close circle. Pull the tail to the inside and weave in all ends.

Block as desired. See page 12 for wet blocking technique.

Go on adventures!

KEY

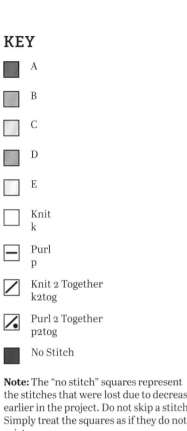

■	A
■	B
■	C
■	D
■	E
□	Knit k
—	Purl p
◿	Knit 2 Together k2tog
◿	Purl 2 Together p2tog
■	No Stitch

Note: The "no stitch" squares represent the stitches that were lost due to decreases earlier in the project. Do not skip a stitch. Simply treat the squares as if they do not exist.

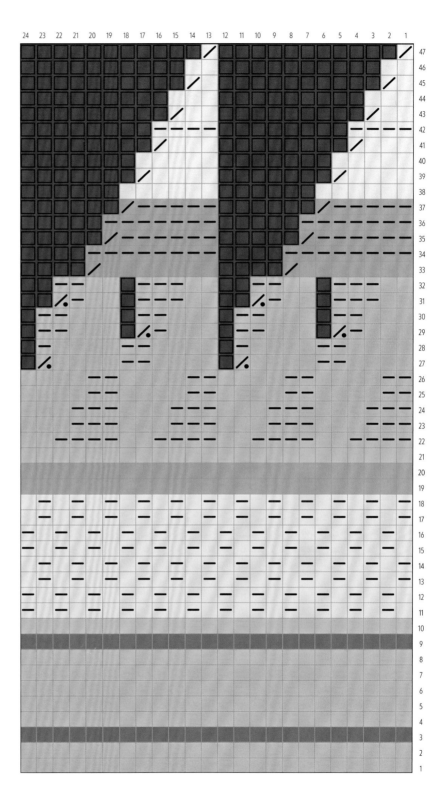

Grand Teton

WYOMING

The magnificent and awe-inspiring Teton Range is a spectacular sight at any time of year, but it is especially magical in early summer when the wildflowers brighten the meadows and hillsides. The contrast in color is stunning! This beanie uses multiple colors to capture this iconic scene from the rich brown soil to the cloud-studded sky. Simple French knot flowers add a pop of summertime color.

SIZE

One size fits an average adult size head (approx. 19 in. / 48 cm to 22 in. / 56 cm).

YARN

Stunning String Studio Legacy Worsted:

- **A:** Pine Cone (25 g / 50 yd. / 46 m)
- **B:** Deep Forest (13 g / 26 yd. / 24 m)
- **C:** Dragon Green (13 g / 26 yd. / 24 m)
- **D:** Charcoal (13 g / 26 yd. / 24 m)
- **E:** Natural (25 g / 50 yd. / 46 m)
- **F:** Big Sky (13 g / 26 yd. / 24 m)

Or other worsted weight (#4) yarn in seven colors.

Optional: Approximately 6 to 8 yards of any yellow yarn for embroidery of flowers

NEEDLES

- US size 5 / 3.75 mm, 16 in. long circular knitting needles
- US size 7 / 4.5 mm, 16 in. long circular knitting needles
- US size 7 / 4.5 mm double pointed needles (DPNs)

Or sizes needed to obtain gauge.

Continued on next page

NOTIONS

- Three stitch markers (two of one color and one of another color)
- Tapestry needle for embroidery and weaving in ends

GAUGE

With larger needles, approximately 9½ stitches = 2 in. in stockinette stitch.

With color A and smaller circular needles, cast on 96 stitches. Place single color marker and join in the round being careful not to twist stitches. Work k1, p1 rib pattern for approximately 1½ to 2 in.

Increase row: *k15, kfb. Rep from * around. 6 increases made—102 sts total.

Switch to larger needles and work chart from right to left beginning on Row 1, bottom right corner. Chart repeats three times around the hat. Use the two remaining stitch markers of another color to mark chart repeats.

Note: In order to avoid long "floats" (strands of yarn on the inside of the hat) do not carry a color more than three to four stitches without twisting the colors around each other in the back of work.

Switch to DPNs when work becomes too small for circular needles.

FINISHING

After Row 45 is complete, cut yarn leaving a 10 in. tail. Using a tapestry needle, weave tail through remaining stitches and pull tightly to close circle. Pull the tail to the inside and weave in all ends.

To add flowers to hat, thread a tapestry needle with a yard or so at a time of yellow yarn. Using a combination of single and double wrap French knots, add flowers as desired around the bottom ¼ to ⅓ of the body of the hat (see photo for approximate placement).

Block as desired. See page 12 for wet blocking technique.

Go on adventures!

KEY

▨	A
▨	B
▨	C
▨	D
☐	E
▨	F
☐	Knit k
◩	Knit 2 Together k2tog
■	No Stitch

Note: The "no stitch" squares represent the stitches that were lost due to decreases earlier in the project. Do not skip a stitch. Simply treat the squares as if they do not exist.

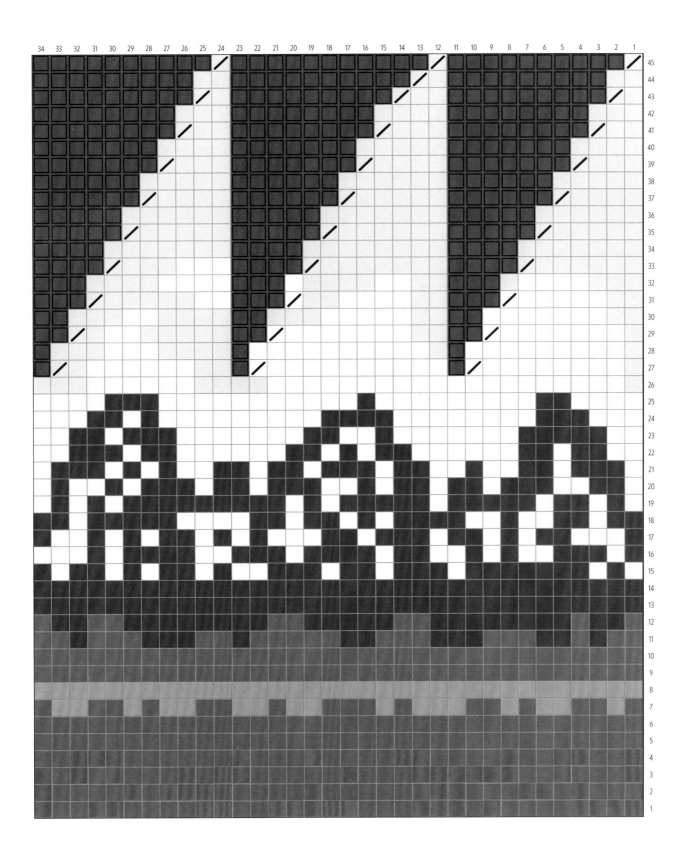

Great Sand Dunes

COLORADO

SIZE

One size fits an average adult size head (approx. 19 in. / 48 cm to 22 in. / 56 cm).

YARN

- **A:** Stunning String Studio Legacy Worsted, Bohemia (25 g / 50 yd. / 46 m)
- **B:** Malabrigo Rios, Ivy (17 g / 35 yd. / 32 m)
- **C:** Peekaboo Yarns Merino Worsted, Zion Blue (10 g / 20 yd. / 18 m)
- **D:** Malabrigo Rios, Fog (25 g / 50 yd. / 46 m)
- **E:** Stunning String Studio Legacy Worsted, Rocky Pass (10 g / 20 yd. / 18 m)
- **F:** Stunning String Studio Legacy Worsted, Big Sky (17 g / 35 yd. / 32 m)

Or other worsted weight yarn (#4) in six colors.

Continued on next page

Amid a landscape of grasslands, forest, wetlands, and alpine tundra in Colorado lies a 30-square-mile dune field with the tallest sand dunes in North America. Visitors to this amazing place can hike, stargaze, sand sled, observe wildlife, go four-wheel driving, and even splash in a creek. But one of the most intriguing aspects of this park is seeing it from a distance where most of the various ecosystems come into view at once. This beanie captures that view from the trees and shrubbery to the massive dunes and up to the Sangre de Cristo Mountains with just a glimpse of seasonal Medano Creek. Randomly spaced cable stitches mimic the giant ever-changing ridges and valleys of the sand.

NEEDLES

- US size 5 / 3.75 mm, 16 in. long circular knitting needles
- US size 7 / 4.5 mm, 16 in. long circular knitting needles
- US size 7 / 4.5 mm double pointed needles (DPNs)

Or sizes needed to obtain gauge.

NOTIONS

- Three stitch markers (two of one color and one of another color)
- Tapestry needle for weaving in ends
- Cable needle (cn)

GAUGE

With larger needles, approximately 9½ stitches = 2 in. in stockinette stitch, blocked.

Note: In order to avoid long "floats" (strands of yarn on the inside of the hat) do not carry a color more than three to four stitches without twisting the colors around each other in the back of work.

Switch to DPNs when work becomes too small for circular needles.

FINISHING

After Row 45 is complete, cut yarn leaving a 10 in. tail. Using a tapestry needle, weave tail through remaining stitches and pull tightly to close circle. Pull the tail to the inside and weave in all ends.

Block as desired. See page 12 for wet blocking technique.

Go on adventures!

KEY

☐	A
◼	B
◼	C
☐	D
◼	E
☐	F

⧖	Cable 4 Front c4f Slip 2 to cn, hold to front. k2, k2 from cn
☐	Knit k
◢	Knit 2 Together k2tog
⊟	Purl p
◼	No Stitch

Note: The "no stitch" squares represent the stitches that were lost due to decreases earlier in the project. Do not skip a stitch. Simply treat the squares as if they do not exist.

With color A and smaller circular needles, cast on 99 stitches. Place single color marker and join in the round being careful not to twist stitches. Work in rib pattern for approximately 1½ in.

Rib pattern: *k2, p2, k1, p2, k1, p1, k1, p1. Repeat from * to end of round.

Switch to larger needles and work chart from right to left beginning on Row 1, bottom right corner. Chart will repeat three times around the hat. Use the two remaining stitch markers of another color to mark chart repeats.

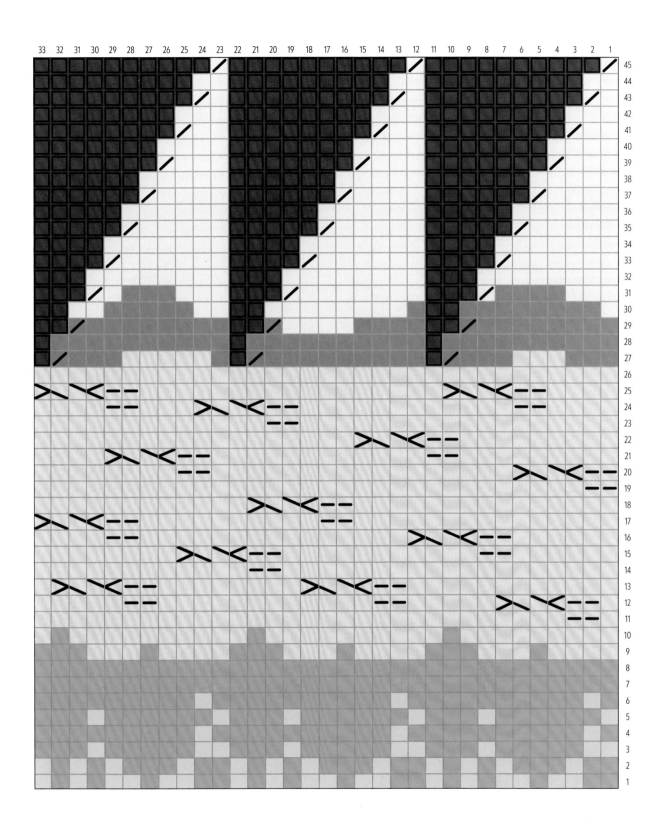

Guadalupe Mountains

TEXAS

Aside from protecting the world's most extensive Permian fossil reef, Guadalupe Mountains offers up canyons, forests, dunes, mountains, and incredible dark skies. From the snakes and lizards of the desert floor to the bears and elk in the mountains, the wildlife is as diverse as the terrain. A strenuous hike to the top of Guadalupe Peak rewards hikers with a breathtaking view—a view from the "Top of Texas." Inspired by the patterns and rich colors of the Southwest, the bottom half of this design features stranded knitting with duplicate stitch accents. The top half features subtle vertical texture, representative of iconic El Capitan and Guadalupe Peaks.

SIZE

One size fits an average adult size head (approx. 19 in. / 48 cm to 22 in. / 56 cm).

YARN

A: Peekaboo Yarns Merino Worsted, Deep Amber (50 g / 100 yd. / 91 m)

B: Stunning String Studio Legacy Worsted, Little Black Dress (15 g / 25 yd. / 23 m)

C: Malabrigo Rios, Natural (15 g / 25 yd. / 23 m)

D: Aly Bee Workshop Merino Worsted, Aquarium (15 g / 25 yd. / 23 m)

E: Aly Bee Workshop Merino Worsted, Honey Bee (15 g / 25 yd. / 23 m)

Or other worsted weight yarn (#4) in five colors.

NEEDLES

- US size 5 / 3.75 mm, 16 in. long circular knitting needles
- US size 7 / 4.5 mm, 16 in. long circular knitting needles
- US size 7 / 4.5 mm double pointed needles (DPNs)

Or sizes needed to obtain gauge.

Continued on next page

NOTIONS

- Three stitch markers (two of one color and one of another color)
- Tapestry needle for weaving in ends

GAUGE

With larger needles, approximately 9½ stitches = 2 in. in stockinette stitch, blocked.

With color A and smaller circular needles, cast on 96 stitches. Place single color marker and join in the round being careful not to twist stitches. Work in k1, p1 rib pattern for approximately 1½ in.

Switch to larger needles and work chart from right to left beginning on Row 1, bottom right corner. Chart repeats three times around the hat. Use the two remaining stitch markers of another color to mark chart repeats.

Note: In order to avoid long "floats" (strands of yarn on the inside of the hat) do not carry a color more than three to four stitches without twisting the colors around each other in the back of work. Do not pull stitches too tightly or your hat will be too small.

Switch to DPNs when work becomes too small for circular needles.

FINISHING

After Row 45 is complete, cut yarn leaving a 10 in. tail. Using a tapestry needle, weave tail through remaining stitches and pull tightly to close circle. Pull the tail to the inside and weave in all ends.

Duplicate stitching: Work duplicate stitch where indicated using color B. I prefer to duplicate stitch after blocking is complete.

Block as desired. See page 12 or wet blocking technique.

Go on adventures!

KEY

■ (dark gray)	A
■ (black)	B
□ (white)	C
■ (gray)	D
■ (light gray)	E
□	Knit k
╱	Knit 2 Together k2tog
D	Duplicate Stitch Work duplicate stitches after all other knitting is complete.
⊟	Purl p
³╱•	Purl 3 Together p3tog
■	No Stitch

Note: The "no stitch" squares represent the stitches that were lost due to decreases earlier in the project. Do not skip a stitch. Simply treat the squares as if they do not exist.

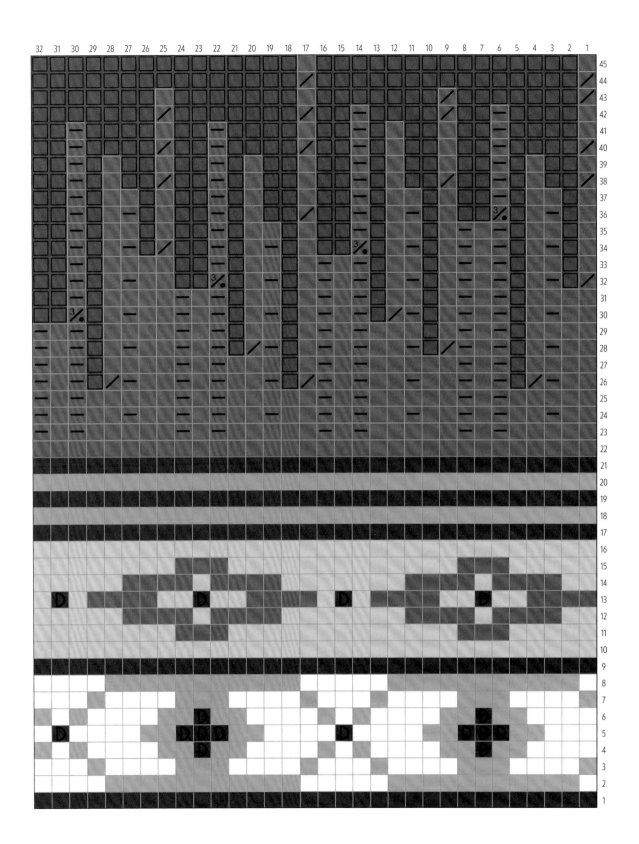

Mesa Verde

COLORADO

A visit to the cliff dwellings carved high into the protected sandstone alcoves of these canyon walls in Colorado is like stepping back in time. The Ancestral Pueblo people who occupied these cliffside communities for generations left behind pottery, tools, and other evidence of skilled workers of every kind. This beanie gets its inspiration not from the cliff dwellings, but from the elaborately decorated black-on-white pottery left behind by the people who once lived there.

SIZE

One size fits an average adult size head (approx. 19 in. / 48 cm to 22 in. / 56 cm).

YARN

Malabrigo Rios:

☐ **A:** Natural (50 g / 100 yd. / 91 m)

▨ **B:** Plomo (50 g / 100 yd. / 91 m)

Or other worsted weight (#4) yarn in two colors.

NEEDLES

- US size 5 / 3.75 mm, 16 in. long circular knitting needles
- US size 7 / 4.5 mm, 16 in. long circular knitting needles
- US size 7 / 4.5 mm double pointed needles (DPNs)

Or sizes needed to obtain gauge.

NOTIONS

- Three stitch markers (two of one color and one of another color)
- Tapestry needle for weaving in ends

GAUGE

With larger needles, approximately 9½ stitches = 2 in. in stockinette stitch.

With color A and smaller circular needles, cast on 96 stitches. Place single color marker and join in the round being careful not to twist stitches.

Work k1, p1 rib pattern for approximately 1½ to 2 in.

Increase row: *k10, M1. Repeat from * to last 6 stitches. k6— 105 sts total.

Switch to larger needles and work chart from right to left beginning on Row 1, bottom right corner. Chart repeats three times around the hat. Use the two remaining stitch markers of another color to mark chart repeats.

Note: In order to avoid long "floats" (strands of yarn on the inside of the hat) do not carry a color more than three to four stitches without twisting the colors around each other in the back of work.

Switch to DPNs when work becomes too small for circular needles.

FINISHING

After Row 47 is complete, cut yarn leaving a 10 in. tail. Using a tapestry needle, weave tail through remaining stitches and pull tightly to close circle. Pull the tail to the inside and weave in all ends.

Block as desired. See page 12 for wet blocking technique.

Go on adventures!

KEY

☐ A

▨ B

☐ Knit k

▨ Knit 2 Together k2tog

■ No Stitch

Note: The "no stitch" squares represent the stitches that were lost due to decreases earlier in the project. Do not skip a stitch. Simply treat the squares as if they do not exist.

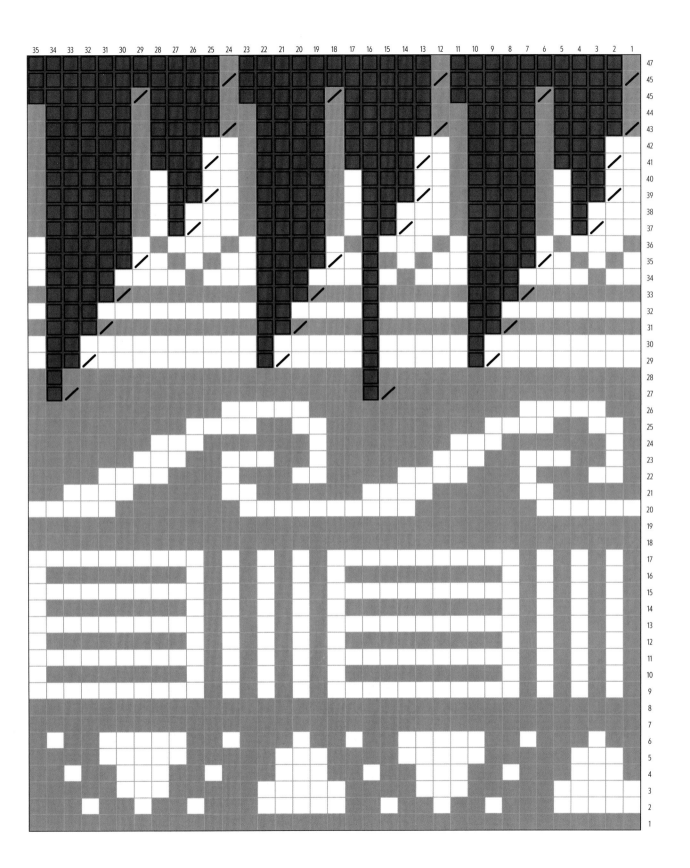

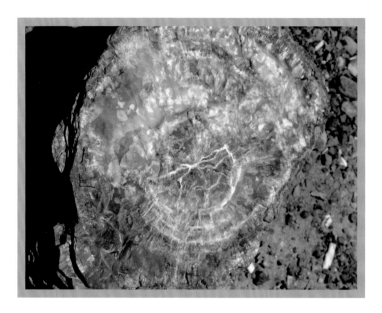

Petrified Forest

ARIZONA

A cross section of a petrified tree reveals a beautiful kaleidoscope of unexpected colors: lavender, red, green, yellow, gray, and more. Remarkably, even after millions of years, most petrified logs still retain the look of bark on the outside. This beanie begins with several rows of seed stitches immediately following the ribbing, which represents the texture of the "bark," before moving on to the smooth bands of color contained in the body of the hat.

SIZE

One size fits an average adult size head (approx. 19 in. / 48 cm to 22 in. / 56 cm).

YARN

Stunning String Studio Legacy Worsted:

- **A:** Rusty Gate (33 g / 66 yd. / 60 m)
- **B:** Wisteria (17 g / 35 yd. / 32 m)
- **C:** Fading Sunlight (13 g / 25 yd. / 23 m)
- **D:** Stone (17 g / 35 yd. / 32 m)
- **E:** Bohemia (17 g / 35 yd. / 32 m)

Or other worsted weight (#4) yarn in five colors.

NEEDLES

- US size 5 / 3.75 mm, 16 in. long circular knitting needles
- US size 7 / 4.5 mm, 16 in. long circular knitting needles
- US size 7 / 4.5 mm double pointed needles (DPNs)

Or sizes needed to obtain gauge.

Continued on next page

NOTIONS

- Three stitch markers (two of one color and one of another color)
- Tapestry needle for weaving in ends

GAUGE

With larger needles, approximately 9 stitches = 2 in. in stockinette stitch.

With color A and smaller circular needles, cast on 96 stitches. Place single color marker and join in the round being careful not to twist stitches. Work k1, p1 rib pattern for approximately 1½ to 2 in.

Increase row: *k16, m1. Rep from * to end of round. 6 increases made—102 sts total.

Switch to larger needles and work chart from right to left beginning on Row 1, bottom right corner. Chart repeats three times around the hat. Use the two remaining stitch markers of another color to mark chart repeats.

Switch to DPNs when work becomes too small for circular needles.

FINISHING

After Row 45 is complete, cut yarn leaving a 10 in. tail. Using a tapestry needle, weave tail through remaining stitches and pull tightly to close circle. Pull the tail to the inside and weave in all ends.

Block as desired. See page 12 for wet blocking technique.

Go on adventures!

KEY

■	A
■	B
□	C
▨	D
▨	E
□	Knit k
◪	Knit 2 Together k2tog
⊟	Purl p
■	No Stitch

Note: The "no stitch" squares represent the stitches that were lost due to decreases earlier in the project. Do not skip a stitch. Simply treat the squares as if they do not exist.

Rocky Mountain

COLORADO

With an elevation that spans 7,600 to 14,259 feet, Rocky Mountain National Park features a diversity of ecosystems that make it a uniquely beautiful and adventurous place to visit. In this design, simple stranded knitting and ten carefully chosen colors take you on a journey to four different lakes in two seasons as you gain elevation up the mountains. Your knitting adventure begins in the subalpine meadows with summertime wildflowers before moving on to Bear Lake and quaking aspens as they appear in the fall. Continue up to Nymph Lake dotted with lily pads and Dream Lake surrounded by evergreens. The final stop is lovely Emerald Lake, near the edge of the timberline with snowcapped peaks nearby.

SIZE

One size fits an average adult size head (approx. 19 in. / 48 cm to 22 in. / 56 cm).

YARN

A: Malabrigo Rios, Ivy (20 g / 40 yd. / 37 m)

B: Malabrigo Rios, Azules (10 g / 20 yd. / 18 m)

C: Peekaboo Yarns Merino Worsted, Giant Kelp (10 g / 20 yd. / 18 m)

D: Peekaboo Yarns Merino Worsted, Cuyahoga Foliage (10 g / 20 yd. / 18 m)

E: Stunning String Studio Legacy Worsted, Big Sky (10 g / 20 yd. / 18 m)

F: Peekaboo Yarns Merino Worsted, Everglades Blue (10 g / 20 yd. / 18 m)

G: Aly Bee Workshop Merino Worsted, Earl Grey (10 g / 20 yd. / 18 m)

H: Peekaboo Yarns Merino Worsted, Tide Pool (10 g / 20 yd. / 18 m)

I: Malabrigo Rios, Natural (10 g / 20 yd. / 18 m)

Or other worsted weight yarn (#4) in ten colors.

Optional: 6 to 8 yards of any color worsted weight yarn for French knot flowers

Continued on next page

NEEDLES

- US size 5 / 3.75 mm, 16 in. long circular knitting needles
- US size 7 / 4.5 mm, 16 in. long circular knitting needles
- US size 7 / 4.5 mm double pointed needles (DPNs)

Or sizes needed to obtain gauge.

NOTIONS

- Three stitch markers (two of one color and one of another color)
- Tapestry needle for weaving in ends, duplicate stitching, and French knots

GAUGE

With larger needles, approximately 9½ stitches = 2 in. in stockinette stitch, blocked.

With color A and smaller circular needles, cast on 96 stitches. Place single color marker and join in the round being careful not to twist stitches. Work in k1, p1 rib pattern for approximately 1½ to 2 in.

Switch to larger needles and work chart from right to left beginning on Row 1, bottom right corner. Chart repeats three times around the hat. Use the two remaining stitch markers of another color to mark chart repeats.

Note: In order to avoid long "floats" (strands of yarn on the inside of the hat) do not carry a color more than three to four stitches without twisting the colors around each other in the back of work. Do NOT pull your floats too tightly or your hat will be too small. Be sure to spread out your stitches on your right needle every five stitches or so to help avoid pulling too tightly.

Switch to DPNs when work becomes too small for circular needles.

FINISHING

After Row 45 is complete, cut yarn leaving a 10 in. tail. Using a tapestry needle, weave tail through remaining stitches and pull tightly to close circle. Pull the tail to the inside and weave in all ends.

Optional: Using any color of yarn and French knots, add flowers in the "meadow" randomly placed near the top of the ribbing and across Row 1 around the hat.

Optional: Using color C, add a few lily pads to the second lake from the bottom using duplicate stitch. See photos for placement inspiration.

Block as desired. See page 12 for wet blocking technique.

Go on adventures!

KEY

▨	A
▨	B
▨	C
▨	D
▨	E
▨	F
▨	G
▨	H
☐	I
☐	Knit k
◪	Knit 2 Together k2tog
■	No Stitch

Note: The "no stitch" squares represent the stitches that were lost due to decreases earlier in the project. Do not skip a stitch. Simply treat the squares as if they do not exist.

Saguaro

ARIZONA

The image of a giant saguaro cactus against a desert sky is synonymous with the American West, and rightly so. These giant plants with arms that seem to be reaching for the sky are pictured in nearly every TV show or movie about the Old West. This beanie captures that spirit on a bright sunny day in springtime with optional embroidered blooms added once the knitting is complete. For a completely different look, create a sunset version with black saguaros silhouetted against a colorful sky.

SIZE

One size fits an average adult size head (approx. 19 in. / 48 cm to 22 in. / 56 cm).

YARN

Daytime Version

A: Malabrigo Rios, Ivy (50 g / 100 yd. / 91 m)

B: Stunning String Studio, Cloudy Sky (50 g / 100 yd. / 91 m)

Several yards each of any white and yellow yarn for embroidering flowers.

Sunset Version (no flowers)

A: Stunning String Studio, Little Black Dress (50 g / 100 yd. / 91 m)

B: Malabrigo Rios, Archangel (50 g / 100 yd. / 91 m)

Or other worsted weight yarn (#4) in two colors.

NEEDLES

- US size 5 / 3.75 mm, 16 in. long circular knitting needles
- US size 7 / 4.5 mm, 16 in. long circular knitting needles
- US size 7 / 4.5 mm double pointed needles (DPNs)

Or sizes needed to obtain gauge.

Continued on next page

NOTIONS

- Three stitch markers (two of one color and one of another color)
- Tapestry needle for weaving in ends and embroidery

GAUGE

With larger needles, approximately 9½ stitches = 2 in. in stockinette stitch, blocked.

With color A and smaller circular needles, cast on 96 stitches. Place single color marker and join in the round being careful not to twist stitches. Work in k1, p1 rib pattern for approximately 1½ in.

Switch to larger needles and work chart from right to left beginning on Row 1, bottom right corner. Chart repeats three times around the hat. Use the two remaining stitch markers of another color to mark chart repeats.

Note: In order to avoid long "floats" (strands of yarn on the inside of the hat) do not carry a color more than three to four stitches without twisting the colors around each other in the back of work. Do not pull stitches too tightly or your hat will be too small.

Switch to DPNs when work becomes too small for circular needles.

FINISHING

After Row 45 is complete, cut yarn leaving a 10 in. tail. Using a tapestry needle, weave tail through remaining stitches and pull tightly to close circle. Pull the tail to the inside and weave in all ends.

Block as desired. See page 12 for wet blocking technique.

Optional: Using photos as a guide, add blooms on some of the cacti using free-form embroidery stitches.

Go on adventures!

KEY

▣	A
☐	B
☐	Knit k
⧄	Knit 2 Together k2tog
■	No Stitch

Note: The "no stitch" squares represent the stitches that were lost due to decreases earlier in the project. Do not skip a stitch. Simply treat the squares as if they do not exist.

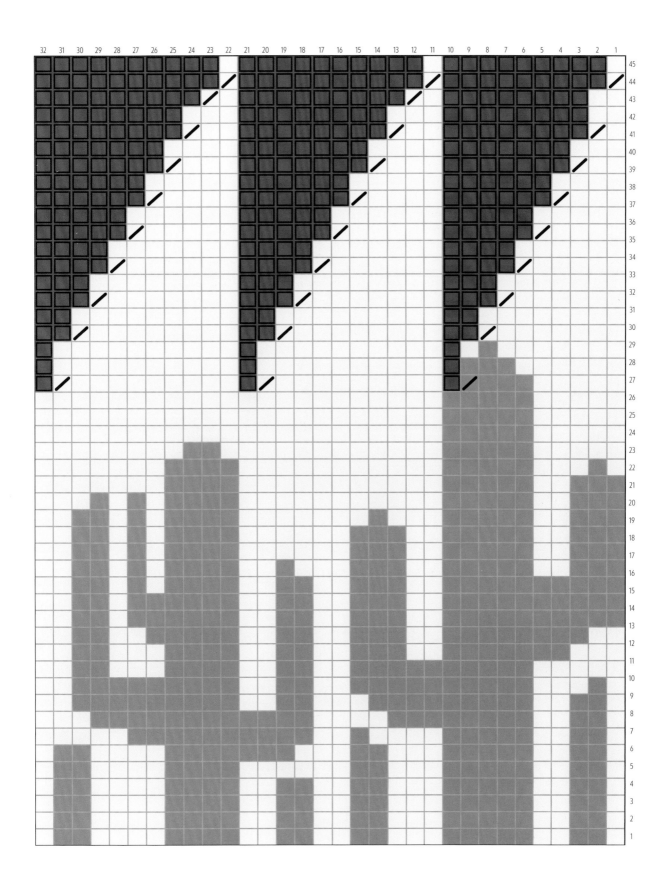

White Sands

NEW MEXICO

White Sands National Park encompasses 275 square miles of the largest gypsum dune field in the world. The sand is so white that most visitors say it looks like snow. Inspired by the texture of windswept ripples of sand and shadow, this beanie features an unusual raised-stitch pattern with small amounts of gray amid a sea of white, resulting in a surprisingly thick and warm hat. For a bit of whimsy, add an optional fluffy green pom-pom to represent the iconic soaptree yucca.

SIZE

One size fits an average adult size head (approx. 19 in. / 48 cm to 22 in. / 56 cm).

YARN

☐ **A:** Lion Brand Basic Stitch, White (100 g / 185 yd. / 170 m)

☐ **B:** Lion Brand Heartland, Mount Rainier (33 g / 66 yd. / 60 m)

Or other worsted weight yarn (#4) in two colors.

Optional Pom-Pom: Peekaboo Yarns Merino Worsted, Kiwi (approx. 10 g / 20 yd. / 18 m)

NEEDLES

- US size 5 / 3.75 mm, 16 in. long circular knitting needles
- US size 7 / 4.5 mm, 16 in. long circular knitting needles
- US size 7 / 4.5 mm double pointed needles (DPNs)

Or sizes needed to obtain gauge.

Continued on next page

NOTIONS

- Four stitch markers (three of one color and one of another color)
- Tapestry needle for weaving in ends

GAUGE

With larger needles, approximately 9½ stitches = 2 in. in stockinette stitch, blocked.

With color A and smaller circular needles, cast on 96 stitches. Place single color marker and join in the round being careful not to twist stitches. Work in k1 tbl (through back loop), p1 rib pattern for approximately 1½ in.

Switch to larger needles and work chart from right to left beginning on Row 1, bottom right corner. Chart repeats four times around the hat. Use the three remaining stitch markers of another color to mark chart repeats. These become especially helpful once you begin the decrease rows.

Important Notes

- Do not cut yarn while switching colors between A and B throughout pattern. Simply carry the colors up the inside of the hat.

- If you will NOT be including a soaptree yucca pom-pom, continue using only white from Row 66 forward as the additional "shadow" is not needed. If you DO plan on including the pom-pom, these

two rows of gray (Rows 66 and 67) create a nice little shadow under the soaptree yucca.

- **Switch to DPNs** when work becomes too small for circular needles.

FINISHING

After Row 69 is complete, cut yarn leaving a 10 in. tail. Using a tapestry needle, weave tail through remaining stitches and pull tightly to close circle. Pull the tail to the inside and weave in all ends.

Block as desired. See page 12 for wet blocking technique.

Using green 4-ply yarn, make a not-so-perfect pom-pom using your preferred method. Fluff it, shape it, or separate the plies to resemble a soaptree yucca plant. Sew onto top of hat.

Go on adventures!

KEY

☐ A

▨ B

☐ Knit
   k

◪ Knit 2 Together
   k2tog

⊗ Sand Ripple Rows
   *With right-hand needle, reach to
   the back side of work. Pick up and lift
   horizontal bar 4 stitches below (the
   first gray bar you see). Place on left
   hand needle and knit together with
   next stitch. Repeat from * around.

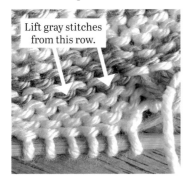

Lift gray stitches
from this row.

■ No Stitch

Note: The "no stitch" squares represent
the stitches that were lost due to decreases
earlier in the project. Do not skip a stitch.
Simply treat the squares as if they do not
exist.

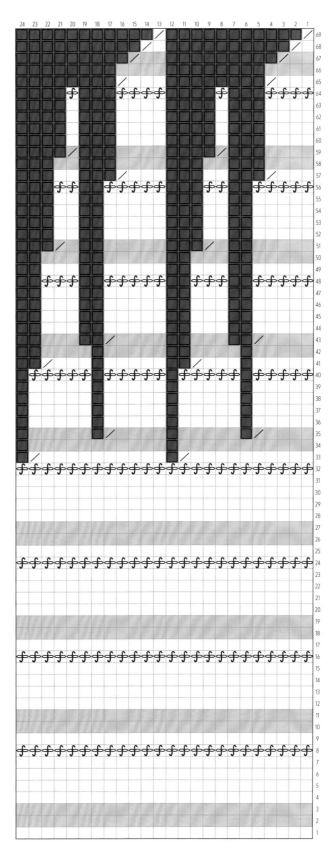

Yellowstone

WYOMING

This colorful beanie is inspired by the beautiful Grand Prismatic Spring, one of the most recognizable features in Yellowstone National Park. The carefully chosen shades represent the spectacular colors of the spring from the grayish-white earth of its surroundings to the deep blue in the center, while the Fair Isle motif itself is a nod to the cold Wyoming winters. An optional wispy white pom-pom represents the steam rising from the hot spring. Whether you choose the traditional colors of the beautiful spring itself or another combination of favorite colors, this pattern knits up fairly quickly and is easy enough for beginners.

SIZE

One size fits an average adult size head (approx. 19 in. / 48 cm to 22 in. / 56 cm).

YARN

A: Stunning String Studio Legacy Worsted, Beach Sand (33 g /66 yd. / 60 m)

B: Malabrigo Rios, Glazed Carrot (13 g / 25 yd. / 23 m)

C: Stunning String Studio Legacy Worsted, Goldenrod (13 g / 25 yd. / 23 m)

D: Stunning String Studio Legacy Worsted, Pasture (13 g / 25 yd. / 23 m)

E: Stunning String Studio Legacy Worsted, Geyser (33 g / 66 yd. / 60 m)

Or other worsted weight (#4) in five colors.

Optional Pom-Pom: Several yards of white 4-ply yarn

NEEDLES

- US size 5 / 3.75 mm, 16 in. long circular knitting needles
- US size 7 / 4.5 mm, 16 in. long circular knitting needles
- US size 7 / 4.5 mm double pointed needles (DPNs)

Or sizes needed to obtain gauge.

Continued on next page

NOTIONS

- Four stitch markers (three of one color and one of another color)
- Tapestry needle for weaving in ends

GAUGE

With larger needles, approximately 9½ stitches = 2 in. in stockinette stitch, blocked.

With color A and smaller circular needles, cast on 96 stitches. Place single color marker and join in the round being careful not to twist stitches. Work k1, p1 rib pattern for approximately 1½ to 2 in.

Switch to larger needles and work chart from right to left beginning on Row 1, bottom right corner. Chart repeats four times around the hat. Use the three remaining stitch markers of another color to mark chart repeats.

Note: In order to avoid long "floats" (strands of yarn on the inside of the hat) do not carry a color more than three to four stitches without twisting the colors around each other in the back of work.

Switch to DPNs when work becomes too small for circular needles.

FINISHING

After Row 45 is complete, cut yarn leaving a 10 in. tail. Using a tapestry needle, weave tail through remaining stitches and pull tightly to close circle. Pull the tail to the inside and weave in all ends.

Block as desired. See page 12 for wet blocking technique.

Optional pom-pom: Using white 4-ply yarn, make a not-so-perfect pom-pom using your preferred method. Separate strands of yarn to simulate the "wispiness" of the steam above the hot spring. Sew onto top of hat.

Go on adventures!

KEY

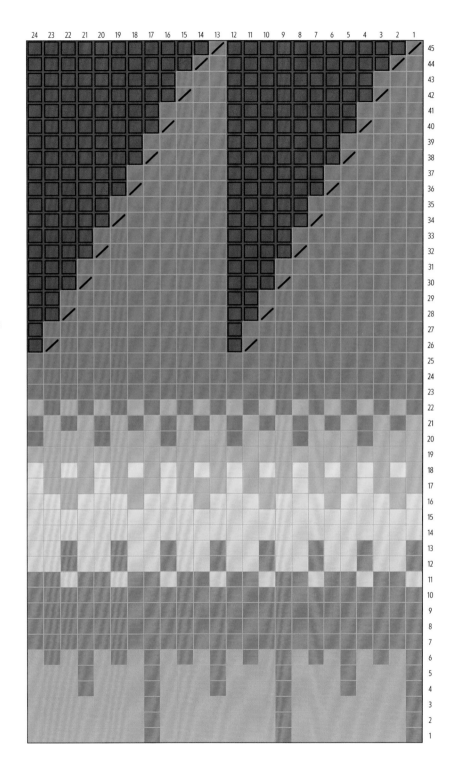

A	
B	
C	
D	
E	
	Knit k
/	Knit 2 Together k2tog
	No Stitch

Note: The "no stitch" squares represent the stitches that were lost due to decreases earlier in the project. Do not skip a stitch. Simply treat the squares as if they do not exist.

Zion

UTAH

Of the 229 square miles that make up Zion National Park, most visitors spend their time in the long narrow canyon that makes this park so popular. The spectacular reds and oranges of the canyon walls, the green of plants and trees and the blues of sky and water create an unforgettable and beloved scene. Whether you're hiking the famous Narrows, Angels Landing, or Emerald Pools trails or simply picnicking along the river, the canyon surrounds you in a palette of warmth and beauty. This textured and colorful design takes you from a forest of cottonwood trees and up the canyon walls to the dark "desert varnish" that paints the orange sandstone. Near the base of the hat, the Virgin River runs throughout—a reminder of the ever-present force still shaping the canyon today.

SIZE

One size fits an average adult size head (approx. 19 in. / 48 cm to 22 in. / 56 cm).

YARN

- **A:** Malabrigo Rios, Camel (20 g / 40 yd. / 37 m)
- **B:** Malabrigo Rios, Ivy (33 g / 66 yd. / 60 m)
- **C:** Peekaboo Yarns Merino Worsted, Tide Pool (10 g / 20 yd. / 18 m)
- **D:** Peekaboo Yarns Merino Worsted, Red Rock West (17 g / 35 yd. / 32 m)
- **E:** Peekaboo Yarns Merino Worsted, Yam (17 g / 35 yd. / 32 m)
- **F:** Malabrigo Rios, Coco (13 g / 25 yd. / 23 m)

Or other worsted weight yarn (#4) in six colors.

NEEDLES

- US size 5 / 3.75 mm, 16 in. long circular knitting needles
- US size 7 / 4.5 mm, 16 in. long circular knitting needles
- US size 7 / 4.5 mm double pointed needles (DPNs)

Or sizes needed to obtain gauge.

Continued on next page

NOTIONS

- Three stitch markers (two of one color and one of another color)
- Tapestry needle for weaving in ends

GAUGE

With larger needles, approximately 9½ stitches = 2 in. in stockinette stitch, blocked.

With color A and smaller circular needles, cast on 96 stitches. Place single color marker and join in the round being careful not to twist stitches. Work in k1, p1 rib pattern for approximately 1½ in.

Increase row: *k31, knit in front and back of next stitch. Repeat from * to end of round. 3 increases made—99 sts total.

Switch to larger needles and work chart from right to left beginning on Row 1, bottom right corner. Chart repeats three times around the hat. Use the two remaining stitch markers of another color to mark chart repeats.

Note: In order to avoid long "floats" (strands of yarn on the inside of the hat) do not carry a color more than three to four stitches without twisting the colors around each other in the back of work. Do not pull stitches too tightly or your hat will be too small.

Switch to DPNs when work becomes too small for circular needles.

FINISHING

After Row 45 is complete, cut yarn leaving a 10 in. tail. Using a tapestry needle, weave tail through remaining stitches and pull tightly to close circle. Pull the tail to the inside and weave in all ends.

Block as desired. See page 12 for wet blocking technique.

Go on adventures!

KEY

▨	A
▨	B
▨	C
▨	D
▨	E
■	F
●	Bobble Stitch (p1, k1, p1, k1) into next stitch, then lift 2nd, 3rd, and 4th stitches over first stitch, one at a time.
☐	Knit k
╱	Knit 2 Together k2tog
⊟	Purl p
☑	Slip Pearlwise with Yarn in Front sl wyif
■	No Stitch

Note: The "no stitch" squares represent the stitches that were lost due to decreases earlier in the project. Do not skip a stitch. Simply treat the squares as if they do not exist.

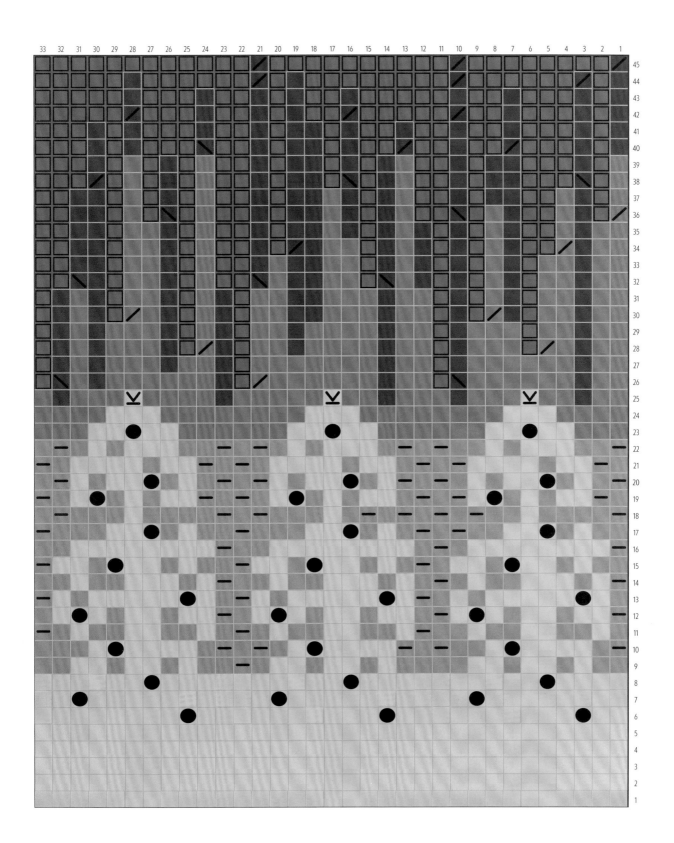

American Samoa

AMERICAN SAMOA

Looking for an American national park in the heart of the South Pacific? Look no further! Rainforests, remote sand beaches, exotic plants and animals, coral reefs, amazing vistas, and some of the tallest sea cliffs in the world await adventurous visitors to this tropical paradise. This design captures one of the many beautiful scenes found throughout the park: colorful plumerias on the coast and waves lapping against the shores of the emerald cliffs of Pola Island.

SIZE

One size fits an average adult size head (approx. 19 in. / 48 cm to 22 in. / 56 cm).

YARN

A: Manos Del Uruguay Alegria Grande, Olive (25 g / 50 yd. / 46 m)

B: Peekaboo Yarns Merino Worsted, Biscayne Blue (20 g / 40 yd. / 37 m)

C: Malabrigo Rios, Natural (17 g / 35 yd. / 32 m)

D: Polka Dot Sheep Whitefish Worsted, River Rock (17 g / 35 yd. / 32 m)

E: Aly Bee Workshop Merino Worsted, Fresh Cut (20 g / 40 yd. / 37 m)

F: Aly Bee Workshop, Merino Worsted, Glass Slipper (20 g / 40 yd. / 37 m)

Or other worsted weight yarn (#4) in six colors (plus flower colors).

NEEDLES

- US size 5 / 3.75 mm, 16 in. long circular knitting needles
- US size 7 / 4.5 mm, 16 in. long circular knitting needles
- US size 7 / 4.5 mm double pointed needles (DPNs)

Or sizes needed to obtain gauge.

Continued on next page

NOTIONS

- Three stitch markers (two of one color and one of another color)
- Tapestry needle for weaving in ends, duplicate stitching, and embroidering flowers

GAUGE

With larger needles, approximately 9½ stitches = 2 in. in stockinette stitch, blocked.

With smaller circular needles, cast on 96 stitches. Place single color marker and join in the round being careful not to twist stitches. Work in k1, p1 rib pattern for approximately 1½ in.

Switch to larger needles and work chart from right to left beginning on Row 1, bottom right corner. Chart repeats three times around the hat. Use the two remaining stitch markers of another color to mark chart repeats.

Note: In order to avoid long "floats" (strands of yarn on the inside of the hat) do not carry a color more than three to four stitches without twisting the colors around each other in the back of work.

Note: No need to carry slip stitch color across the back of the work. Simply knit with the other colors in that row and slip these stitches as you come to them.

Switch to DPNs when work becomes too small for circular needles.

FINISHING

After Row 45 is complete, cut yarn leaving a 10 in. tail. Using a tapestry needle, weave tail through remaining stitches and pull tightly to close circle. Pull the tail to the inside and weave in all ends.

Block as desired. See page 12 for wet blocking technique.

Work duplicate stitches.

Optional Flowers: With a tapestry needle and pink, yellow, or orange yarn (or all three), add plumerias to your hat using single and double wrap French knots.

Go on adventures!

KEY

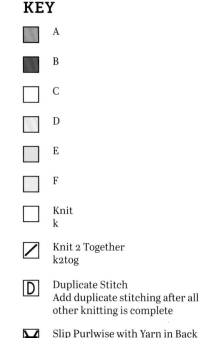

▨	A
▨	B
☐	C
▨	D
▨	E
▨	F
☐	Knit k
◺	Knit 2 Together k2tog
D	Duplicate Stitch Add duplicate stitching after all other knitting is complete
⊻	Slip Purlwise with Yarn in Back sl wyib
◹	Slip Slip Knit ssk
■	No Stitch

Note: The "no stitch" squares represent the stitches that were lost due to decreases earlier in the project. Do not skip a stitch. Simply treat the squares as if they do not exist.

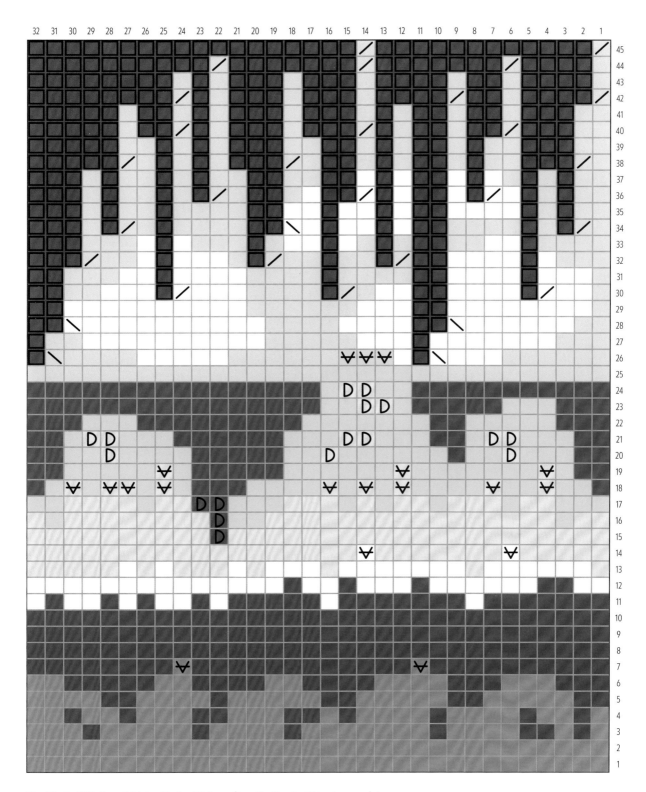

Duplicate Stitches: Add duplicate stitches after all other knitting is complete. In the meantime, knit these stitches using color D in Rows 15 to 17 and color E in Rows 20 to 24.

Channel Islands

CALIFORNIA

From diving and kayaking to hiking and camping, it's the landscapes above *and* below the water that draw thousands of adventurous visitors to these amazing islands off the coast of Southern California each year. Wildflowers in the spring add even more color and dimension to the already stunning views. This beanie uses subtly textured stitches and the beautiful colors of the sea and the land to create a stylized landscape that's fun to knit and wear!

SIZE

One size fits an average adult size head (approx. 19 in. / 48 cm to 22 in. / 56 cm).

YARN

Peekaboo Yarns Merino Worsted:

- **A:** Giant Kelp (33 g / 67 yd. / 61 m.)
- **B:** Pacific (25 g / 50 yd. / 46 m)
- **C:** Whitewater (10 g / 20 yd. / 18 m)
- **D:** Anacapa Island (20 g / 40 yd. / 37 m)
- **E:** Yellow Coreopsis (10 g / 20 yd. / 18 m)

Or other worsted weight yarn (#4) in five colors.

NEEDLES

- US size 5 / 3.75 mm, 16 in. long circular knitting needles
- US size 7 / 4.5 mm, 16 in. long circular knitting needles
- US size 7 / 4.5 mm double pointed needles (DPNs)

Or sizes needed to obtain gauge.

Continued on next page

NOTIONS

- Three stitch markers (two of one color and one of another color)
- Tapestry needle for weaving in ends

GAUGE

With larger needles, approximately 9½ stitches = 2 in. in stockinette stitch, blocked.

With color A and smaller circular needles, cast on 96 stitches. Place single color marker and join in the round being careful not to twist stitches. Work in k1, p1 rib pattern for approximately 1½ to 2 in.

Increase row: *k32, M1, repeat from * to end of round—99 sts total.

Switch to larger needles and work chart from right to left beginning on Row 1, bottom right corner. Chart repeats three times around the hat. Use the two remaining stitch

markers of another color to mark chart repeats.

Note: In order to avoid long "floats" (strands of yarn on the inside of the hat) do not carry a color more than three to four stitches without twisting the colors around each other in the back of work. Do NOT pull your floats too tightly or your hat will be too small. Be sure to spread out your stitches on your right needle every five stitches or so to help avoid pulling too tightly.

Switch to DPNs when work becomes too small for circular needles.

FINISHING

After Row 46 is complete, cut yarn leaving a 10 in. tail. Using a tapestry needle, weave tail through remaining stitches and pull tightly to close circle. Pull the tail to the inside and weave in all ends.

Block as desired. See page 12 for wet blocking technique.

Go on adventures!

KEY

☐	A
☐	B
☐	C
☐	D
☐	E
☒	**Left Crossover** With yarn in front, sl 1 purlwise, p1, wrap yarn over needle from back to front, pass the sl st over the p1 and the wrap.
☐	Knit k
◻	Knit 2 Together k2tog
◻	Knit in Front and Back of Same Stitch kfb
⊟	Purl p
■	No Stitch

Note: The "no stitch" squares represent the stitches that were lost due to decreases earlier in the project. Do not skip a stitch. Simply treat the squares as if they do not exist.

Crater Lake

OREGON

At a depth of 1,943 feet, Crater Lake is the deepest lake in the United States and one of the purest in the world. The water in the lake only comes from snow and rain; there are no rivers or streams that feed into the lake carrying sediments and other debris with them. This perfect combination of depth and purity atop an ancient volcano creates a blue so stunning, it almost seems unreal. This beanie captures the unforgettable scene of forest, crater rim, azure water, and, of course, lovely Wizard Island, the tip of the volcano.

SIZE

One size fits an average adult size head (approx. 19 in. / 48 cm to 22 in. / 56 cm).

YARN

- **A:** Malabrigo Rios, Vaa (50 g / 100 yd. / 91 m)
- **B:** Dragonfly Fibers Valkyrie, Winter Woods (25 g / 50 yd. / 46 m)
- **C:** Malabrigo Rios, Reflecting Pool (12 g / 24 yd. / 22 m)
- **D:** Malabrigo Rios, Matisse Blue (20 g / 40 yd. / 37 m)

Or other worsted weight (#4) yarn in four colors.

NEEDLES

- US size 5 / 3.75 mm, 16 in. long circular knitting needles
- US size 7 / 4.5 mm, 16 in. long circular knitting needles
- US size 7 / 4.5 mm double pointed needles (DPNs)

Or sizes needed to obtain gauge.

NOTIONS

- Three stitch markers (two of one color and one of another color)
- Tapestry needle for weaving in ends

GAUGE

With larger needles, approximately 9½ stitches = 2 in. in stockinette stitch, blocked.

With color A and smaller circular needles, cast on 96 stitches. Place single color marker and join in the round being careful not to twist stitches.

Work k1, p1 rib pattern for approximately 4 in.

Increase row: *k32, M1, repeat from * to end of round—99 sts total.

Switch to larger needles and work chart from right to left beginning on Row 1, bottom right corner. Chart repeats three times around the hat. Use the two remaining stitch markers of another color to mark chart repeats.

Note: In order to avoid long "floats" (strands of yarn on the inside of the hat) do not carry a color more than three to four stitches without twisting the colors around each other in the back of work.

Switch to DPNs when work becomes too small for circular needles.

FINISHING

After Row 46 is complete, cut yarn leaving a 10 in. tail. Using a tapestry needle, weave tail through remaining stitches and pull tightly to close circle. Pull the tail to the inside and weave in all ends.

Block as desired. See page 12 for wet blocking technique.

Go on adventures!

KEY

- ■ A
- ■ B
- ■ C
- ■ D
- ☐ Knit k
- ⧄ Knit 2 Together k2tog
- ■ No Stitch

Note: The "no stitch" squares represent the stitches that were lost due to decreases earlier in the project. Do not skip a stitch. Simply treat the squares as if they do not exist.

Death Valley

CALIFORNIA

At first glance, the saltwater flats of Death Valley's Badwater Basin, which is the lowest point in the United States at 282 feet below sea level, look like miles of flat nothingness. But once you venture beyond the beaten path for a while, you'll find a surreal and almost otherworldly landscape of salt crystals pushing through the crust to form chaotic and beautiful patterns. This beanie uses single-stitch traveling cables along with strategically placed increases and decreases to recreate the "triple junctions" that naturally occur as the salt crystals expand. The purposeful asymmetry of the formations gives this hat an organic look and feel.

SIZE

One size fits an average adult size head (approx. 19 in. / 48 cm to 22 in. / 56 cm).

YARN

A: Peekaboo Yarns Merino Worsted, Shifting Sands (100 g /200 yd. / 183 m)

Or other worsted weight yarn (#4).

NEEDLES

- US size 5 / 3.75 mm, 16 in. long circular knitting needles
- US size 7 / 4.5 mm, 16 in. long circular knitting needles
- US size 7 / 4.5 mm double pointed needles (DPNs)

Or sizes needed to obtain gauge.

NOTIONS

- Three stitch markers (two of one color and one of another color)
- Cable needle (cn)
- Tapestry needle for weaving in ends

GAUGE

With larger needles, approximately 9½ stitches = 2 in. in stockinette stitch, blocked.

With smaller circular needles, cast on 96 stitches. Place single color marker and join in the round being careful not to twist stitches. Work in k1, p1 rib pattern for approximately 1½ in. to 2 in.

Setup/increase row: *p4, k1, p7, kfb, p5, kfb, p7, k1, p3, kfb, p1. Repeat from * 3 times. 9 increases made—105 sts total.

Switch to larger needles and work chart from right to left beginning on Row 1, bottom right corner. Chart repeats three times around the hat. Use the two remaining stitch markers of another color to mark chart repeats.

Switch to DPNs when work becomes too small for circular needles.

FINISHING

After Row 46 is complete, cut yarn leaving a 10 in. tail. Using a tapestry needle, weave tail through remaining stitches and pull tightly to close circle. Pull the tail to the inside and weave in all ends.

Block as desired. See page 12 for wet blocking technique.

Go on adventures!

KEY

⬚ 1/1 Left Purl Cable
1/1 lpc
S1 to cn, hold in front, p1; k1 from cn

⬚ 1/1 Right Purl Cable
1/1 rpc
S1 to cn, hold in back, k1; p1 from cn

⬚ 2/1 Left Purl Cable
2/1 lpc
S1 to cn, hold in front, p2; k1 from cn

⬚ 2/1 Right Purl Cable
2/1 rpc
S2 to cn, hold in back, k1; p2 from cn

⬚ Knit
k

⬚ Knit 2 Together
k2tog

⬚ Knit Front, Slip Back
kfsb
Knit the stitch without transferring to right needle. Insert needle in back leg, slip both to right needle.

Ⓜ Make 1 Purlwise
M1p
Insert needle from back to front and lift strand between stitch just worked and the next stitch. Purl through front of this strand.

⬚ Rows 10, 24, and 38: Remove marker, sl first stitch (at beginning of 1st chart repeat only). Replace marker. Work chart to last stitch, remove marker, sl stitch to left needle, k2tog, replace marker. On last chart repeat, knit last 2 stitches together.

◎ Row 13 and 14 only: Work pattern to last stitch on Row 13 *(Sl st to right needle, remove marker, place stitch on left needle, replace marker, work pattern to last stitch). Repeat from * two more times. Work last chart repeat as written to end of round.

⬚ Purl
p

⬚ Purl 2 Together
p2tog

⬛ No Stitch

Note: The "no stitch" squares represent the stitches that were lost due to decreases earlier in the project. Do not skip a stitch. Simply treat the squares as if they do not exist.

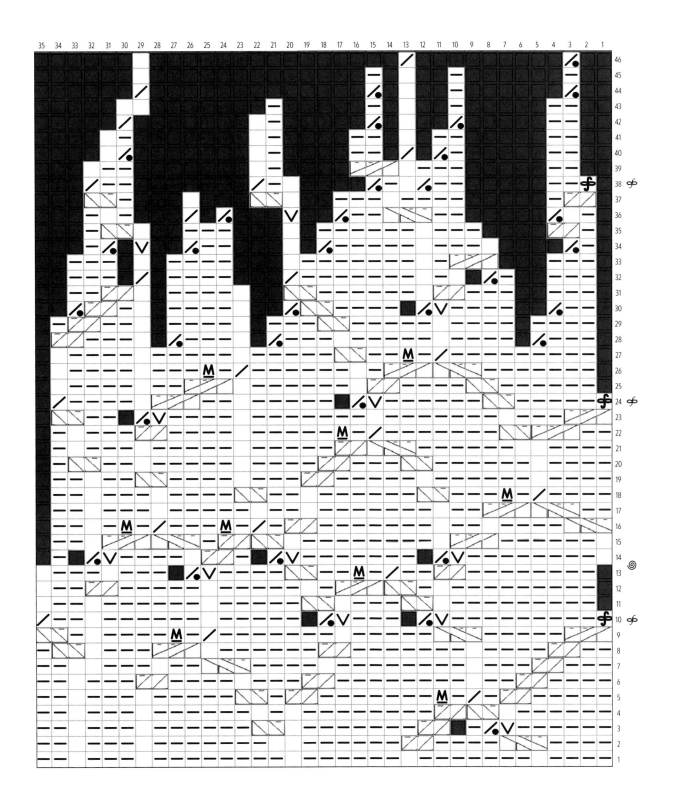

Great Basin

NEVADA

SIZE

One size fits an average adult size head (approx. 19 in. / 48 cm to 22 in. / 56 cm).

YARN

A: Peekaboo Yarns Merino Worsted, Stornoway (50 g / 100 yd. / 91 m)

B: Malabrigo Rios, Azules (50 g / 100 yd. / 91 m)

Or other worsted weight yarn (#4) in two colors.

Optional: Beads of any color for stars

NEEDLES

- US size 5 / 3.75 mm, 16 in. long circular knitting needles
- US size 7 / 4.5 mm, 16 in. long circular knitting needles
- US size 7 / 4.5 mm double pointed needles (DPNs)

Or sizes needed to obtain gauge.

NOTIONS

- Three stitch markers (two of one color and one of another color)
- Tapestry needle for weaving in ends

GAUGE

With larger needles, approximately 9½ stitches = 2 in. stockinette stitch.

Great Basin is a diverse land, from desert and forests to tall peaks to streams that flow inward and never reach the ocean. Visitors can hike to a glacier, stargaze, take a scenic drive, look for pictographs, fish in a creek, see over 800 different plants, and even explore a cave. But one of the most memorable and awe-inspiring experiences is a quiet walk among the oldest trees in the world: the ancient bristlecone pines. These gnarled, twisted, and wind-polished trees can live to be almost 5,000 years old! Using colors that evoke a feeling of solitude at twilight, this beanie combines two of the park's most famous features: bristlecone pines and incredibly dark skies. Add stars to your skyscape using silver or sparkly beads that are knitted in or sewn on afterwards.

With color A and smaller circular needles, cast on 96 stitches. Place single color marker and join in the round being careful not to twist stitches. Work in k1, p1 rib pattern for approximately 1½ in.

Increase row: *k16, m1. Rep from * to end of round. 6 increases made—102 sts total.

Switch to larger needles and work chart from right to left beginning on Row 1, bottom right corner. Chart repeats three times around the hat. Use the two remaining stitch markers of another color to mark chart repeats.

Note: In order to avoid long "floats" (strands of yarn on the inside of the hat) do not carry a color more than three to four stitches without twisting the colors around each other in the back of work. Do NOT pull your floats too tightly or your hat will be too small. Be sure to spread out your stitches on your right needle every five stitches or so to help avoid pulling too tightly.

Switch to DPNs when work becomes too small for circular needles.

Optional "Stars": If desired, add beads to your hat to create stars in the sky. Beads can be added randomly while knitting (using the crochet hook or stringing method) or sewn on after all knitting and blocking is complete. Add as many or as few as you'd like. You can even create your favorite constellation! See photo for star placement inspiration, including the Big Dipper.

FINISHING

After Row 46 is complete, cut yarn leaving a 10 in. tail. Using a tapestry needle, weave tail through remaining stitches and pull tightly to close circle. Pull the tail to the inside and weave in all ends.

Block as desired. See page 12 for wet blocking technique.

Go on adventures!

KEY

■ A

▨ B

□ Knit
k

◸ Knit 2 Together
k2tog

⩒ Slip Purlwise with Yarn in Back
sl wyib

⩒ No Stitch

Note: The "no stitch" squares represent the stitches that were lost due to decreases earlier in the project. Do not skip a stitch. Simply treat the squares as if they do not exist.

Rows 25 to 26 slipped stitches: No need to carry color A across the back of the work.
Simply knit with color B and then slip color A where shown.

Haleakalā

HAWAII

Haleakalā, or the East Maui Volcano (the tallest peak on the island of Maui), stands more than 10,000 feet above sea level and can be spotted from almost everywhere on the island. Since the 1890s, millions of visitors have made the trek up to the cold and windy summit for a moving experience to watch the sunrise over a sea of clouds. In this design, custom dyed colors and stranded knitting capture the warmth and serenity of the scene in a cozy hat suitable for your next trip to the top of a volcano or any place closer to home.

SIZE

One size fits an average adult size head (approx. 19 in. / 48 cm to 22 in. / 56 cm).

YARN

A: Peekaboo Yarns Superwash Merino Worsted, Stornoway (33 g / 66 yd. / 60 m)

B: Peekaboo Yarns Superwash Merino Worsted, Asperitas (33 g / 66 yd. / 60 m)

C: Peekaboo Yarns Superwash Merino Worsted, Cumulus (33 g / 66 yd. / 60 m)

D: Aly Bee Workshop Superwash Merino Worsted, Island Sunrise (13 g / 25 yd. / 23 m)

Or other worsted weight (#4) yarn in four colors.

NEEDLES

- US size 5 / 3.75 mm, 16 in. long circular knitting needles
- US size 7 / 4.5 mm, 16 in. long circular knitting needles
- US size 7 / 4.5 mm double pointed needles (DPNs)

Or sizes needed to obtain gauge.

Continued on next page

NOTIONS

- Three stitch markers (two of one color and one of another color)
- Tapestry needle for weaving in ends

GAUGE

With larger needles, approximately 9½ stitches = 2 in. in stockinette stitch.

FINISHING

After Row 47 is complete, cut yarn leaving a 10 in. tail. Using a tapestry needle, weave tail through remaining stitches and pull tightly to close circle. Pull the tail to the inside and weave in all ends.

Block as desired. See page 12 for wet blocking technique.

Go on adventures!

KEY

▓	A
░	B
▒	C
▒	D
□	Knit k
╱	Knit 2 Together k2tog
⩔	Slip Purlwise with Yarn in Back sl wyib
■	No Stitch

Note: The "no stitch" squares represent the stitches that were lost due to decreases earlier in the project. Do not skip a stitch. Simply treat the squares as if they do not exist.

With smaller circular needles and color A, cast on 96 stitches. Place single color marker and join in the round being careful not to twist stitches. Work k1, p1 rib pattern for approximately 1½ to 2 in.

Increase row: *k31, knit in front and back of next stitch. Repeat from * to end of round—99 sts total.

Switch to larger needles and work chart from right to left beginning on Row 1, bottom right corner. Chart will repeat three times around the hat. Use the two remaining stitch markers of another color to mark chart repeats.

Note: In order to avoid long "floats" (strands of yarn on the inside of the hat) do not carry a color more than four to five stitches without twisting the colors around each other in the back of work.

Switch to DPNs when work becomes too small for circular needles.

Row 9: Do NOT carry color A across the back of the work. Simply knit with colors B and C and then slip color A where shown.

Hawaii Volcanoes

HAWAII

Visitors from around the world are drawn to Hawaii for the lush rainforest, varied wildlife, stunning hikes, and a glimpse at two of the world's most active volcanoes. Periodic eruptions send rivers of lava to the coast where the ocean boils and steams as the 2,192°F (1,200°C) molten lava pours and drips into the sea, forever changing the landscape. . . until the next time. This beanie uses four colors in a Fair Isle "lava-inspired" design.

SIZE

One size fits an average adult size head (approx. 19 in. / 48 cm to 22 in. / 56 cm).

YARN

Stunning String Studio Legacy Worsted:

- **A:** Stained Glass (25 g / 50 yd. / 46 m)
- **B:** Dove (20 g / 40 yd. / 37 m)
- **C:** Lava (20 g / 40 yd. / 37 m)
- **D:** Charcoal (33 g / 66 yd. / 60 m)

Or other worsted weight (#4) yarn in four colors.

NEEDLES

- US size 5 / 3.75 mm, 16 in. long circular knitting needles
- US size 7 / 4.5 mm, 16 in. long circular knitting needles
- US size 7 / 4.5 mm double pointed needles (DPNs)

Or sizes needed to obtain gauge.

NOTIONS

- Four stitch markers (three of one color and one of another color)
- Tapestry needle for weaving in ends

GAUGE

With larger needles, approximately 9½ stitches = 2 in. in stockinette stitch.

With color A and smaller circular needles, cast on 96 stitches. Place single color marker and join in the round being careful not to twist stitches.

Work k1, p1 rib pattern for approximately 1½ to 2 in.

Switch to larger needles and work chart from right to left beginning on Row 1, bottom right corner. Chart will repeat four times around the hat. Use the three remaining stitch markers of another color to mark chart repeats.

Note: In order to avoid long "floats" (strands of yarn on the inside of the hat) do not carry a color more than three to four stitches without twisting the colors around each other in the back of work. Do NOT pull tightly as you knit or hat will be too small.

Switch to DPNs when work becomes too small for circular needles.

FINISHING

After Row 46 is complete, cut yarn leaving a 10 in. tail. Using a tapestry needle, weave tail through remaining stitches and pull tightly to close circle. Pull the tail to the inside and weave in all ends.

Block as desired. See page 12 for wet blocking technique.

Go on adventures!

KEY

⬛	A
⬜	B
⬛	C
⬛	D
⬜	Knit k
◪	Knit 2 Together k2tog
⬛	No Stitch

Note: The "no stitch" squares represent the stitches that were lost due to decreases earlier in the project. Do not skip a stitch. Simply treat the squares as if they do not exist.

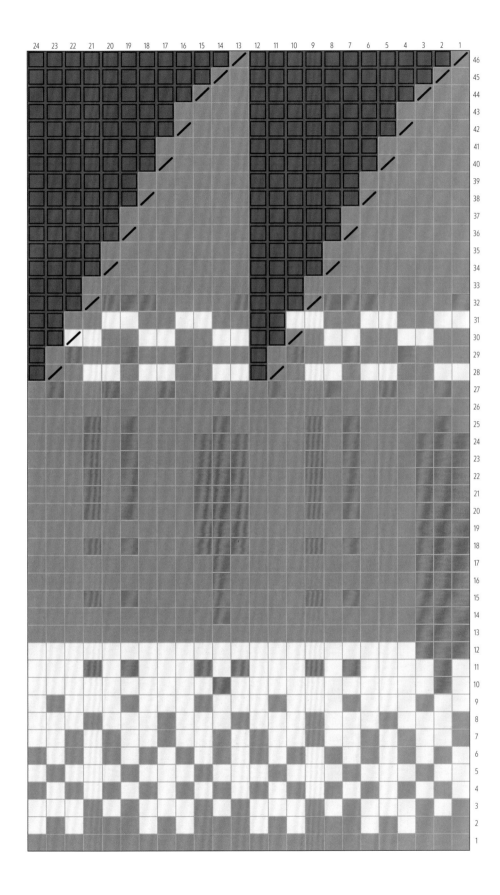

Joshua Tree

CALIFORNIA

If you're ever on a road trip and you spot the characteristic "hairy" branches and spiky green tufts of a Joshua tree, you can only be in one place—the southwestern United States. These unique yucca succulents grow straight out of the desert floor and have spiny arms that reach out in every direction. The two distinct ecosystems of the Mojave and Colorado deserts converge in this park, making it an even more unique place to visit. This fun and whimsical beanie uses a combination of cables and bobbles to create six Joshua trees growing right out of the ribbing of your hat.

SIZE

One size fits an average adult size head (approx. 19 in. / 48 cm to 22 in. / 56 cm).

YARN

A: Lion Brand Heartland, Joshua Tree (1 skein / 251 yds / 230 m)

Or other worsted weight yarn (#4).

NEEDLES

- US size 5 / 3.75 mm, 16 in. long circular knitting needles
- US size 7 / 4.5 mm, 16 in. long circular knitting needles
- US size 7 / 4.5 mm double pointed needles (DPNs)

Or sizes needed to obtain gauge.

NOTIONS

- Three stitch markers (two of one color and one of another color)
- Tapestry needle for weaving in ends
- Cable needle (cn)

GAUGE

With larger needles, approximately 9 stitches = 2 in. in stockinette stitch.

THE PACIFIC WEST REGION   195

With smaller circular needles, cast on 96 stitches. Join in the round being careful not to twist stitches. Work rib pattern for approximately 2 in.

Rib pattern: *(k1, p1) 4 times, k6, (p1, k1) 4 times, p1, K4, (p1, k1) 2 times, p1. Repeat from * 2 more times—96 sts total.

Switch to larger needles and work **main chart** from right to left beginning on Row 1, bottom right corner. Chart repeats three times around the hat. Use the two remaining stitch markers of another color to mark chart repeats.

After Row 31, you should have 24 stitches per chart repeat—72 sts total.

Work **decrease chart** as shown beginning with Row 1, bottom right corner.

Switch to DPNs when work becomes too small for circular needles.

FINISHING

After decrease chart is complete, cut yarn leaving a 10 in. tail. Using a tapestry needle, weave tail through remaining 6 stitches and pull tightly to close circle. Pull the tail to the inside and weave in all ends.

Block as desired. See page 12 for wet blocking technique.

Go on adventures!

KEY

2/1 LPC 2/1 Left Purl Cable
Sl 2 to cn, hold in front, p1; k2 from cn

2/1 RPC 2/1 Right Purl Cable
Sl 1 to cn, hold in back, k2; p1 from cn

2/2 LPC 2/2 Left Purl Cable
Sl 2 to cn, hold in front, p2; k2 from cn

2/2 RC 2/2 Right Cable
Sl 2 to cn, hold in back, k2; k2 from cn

2/2 RPC 2/2 Right Purl Cable
Sl 2 to cn, hold in back, k2; p2 from cn

3/1 LC 3/1 Left Cable
Sl 3 to cn, hold in front, k1; k3 from cn

3/1 LPC 3/1 Left Purl Cable
Sl 3 to cn, hold in front, p1; k3 from cn

Make Bobble
Knit into the front and back of next stitch 2 times, turn, p4, turn, k4, (sl second stitch on the right-hand needle over the first stitch) 3 times.

Knit
k

Purl
p

Purl 2 Together
p2tog

No Stitch

Note: The "no stitch" squares represent the stitches that were lost due to decreases earlier in the project. Do not skip a stitch. Simply treat the squares as if they do not exist.

MAIN CHART

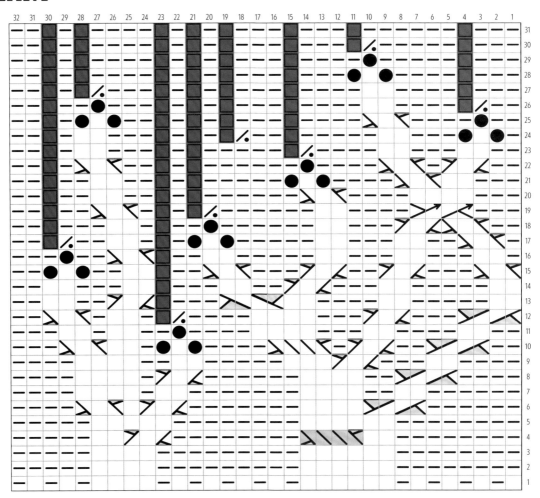

DECREASE CHART

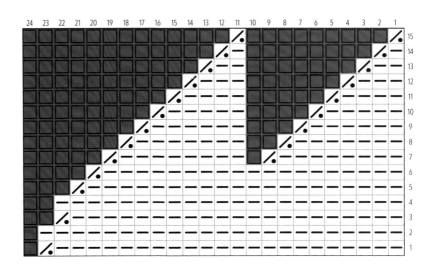

Kings Canyon

CALIFORNIA

Visitors to Kings Canyon are greeted by groves of giant sequoias before entering the spectacular glacially carved canyon with huge granite walls that tower up to 4,000 feet. A single curvy road takes visitors on a precipitous and scenic journey to a place of adventure and outdoor beauty. Inspired by tall granite walls and a hike near Kings River dotted with boulders, this design features earthy colors in simple stranded knitting. Three shades of gray give the illusion of layers of mountains viewed further and further away.

SIZE

One size fits an average adult size head (approx. 19 in. / 48 cm to 22 in. / 56 cm).

YARN

☐ **A:** Aly Bee Workshop Merino Worsted, Fresh Cut (20 g / 40 yd. / 37 m)

☐ **B:** Peekaboo Yarns Merino Worsted, Silvertone (25 g / 50 yd. / 46 m)

☐ **C:** Peekaboo Yarns Merino Worsted, Everglades Blue (10 g / 20 yd. / 18 m)

☐ **D:** Malabrigo Rios, Sand Storm (20 g / 40 yd. / 37 m)

☐ **E:** Malabrigo Rios, Vaa (10 g / 20 yd. / 18 m)

☐ **F:** Peekaboo Yarns Merino Worsted, Classic Silver (20 g / 40 yd. / 37 m)

Or other worsted weight yarn (#4) in six colors.

NEEDLES

- US size 5 / 3.75 mm, 16 in. long circular knitting needles
- US size 7 / 4.5 mm, 16 in. long circular knitting needles
- US size 7 / 4.5 mm double pointed needles (DPNs)

Or sizes needed to obtain gauge.

Continued on next page

NOTIONS

- Three stitch markers (two of one color and one of another color)
- Tapestry needle for weaving in ends

GAUGE

With larger needles, approximately 9½ stitches = 2 in. in stockinette stitch.

With color A and smaller circular needles, cast on 96 stitches. Place single color marker and join in the round being careful not to twist stitches. Work in k1, p1 rib pattern for approximately 1½ in.

Switch to larger needles and work chart from right to left beginning on Row 1, bottom right corner. Chart repeats three times around the hat. Use the two remaining stitch markers of another color to mark chart repeats.

Note: In order to avoid long "floats" (strands of yarn on the inside of the hat) do not carry a color more than three to four stitches without twisting the colors around each other in the back of work. Do NOT pull your floats too tightly or your hat will be too small. Be sure to spread out your stitches on your right needle every five stitches or so to help avoid pulling too tightly.

Switch to DPNs when work becomes too small for circular needles.

FINISHING

After Row 47 is complete, cut yarn leaving a 10 in. tail. Using a tapestry needle, weave tail through remaining stitches and pull tightly to close circle. Pull the tail to the inside and weave in all ends.

Block as desired. See page 12 for wet blocking technique.

Go on adventures!

KEY

- A
- B
- C
- D
- E
- F

Knit
k

Knit 2 Together
k2tog

Slip Purlwise with Yarn in Back
sl wyib

No Stitch

Note: The "no stitch" squares represent the stitches that were lost due to decreases earlier in the project. Do not skip a stitch. Simply treat the squares as if they do not exist.

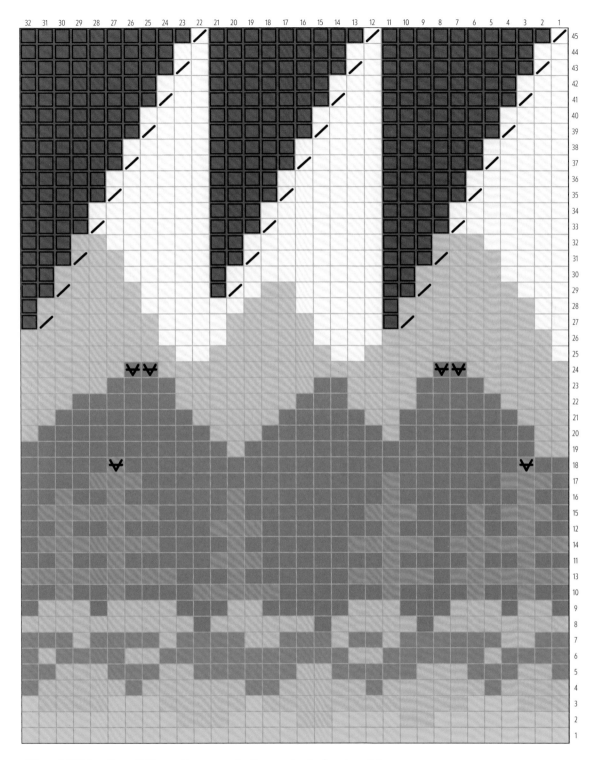

Slipped Stitches Row 18: No need to carry color E across back of work on this row. Knit with color D across row and then slip color E where indicated.

Slipped Stitches Row 24: No need to carry color D across back of work on this row. Knit with color B across row and then slip color D where indicated.

Lassen Volcanic

CALIFORNIA

The continuous bubbling movement and plopping sounds of mud pots at Lassen Volcanic National Park are fascinating and mesmerizing. This constant geothermal activity creates circular patterns in the mud that shift and move next to and on top of each other as steam escapes up to the surface. In this fun-to-knit beanie, single-stitch cables and textured stitches recreate the uneven circular patterns while the optional double-wide ribbing keeps your ears cozy and warm.

SIZE

One size fits an average adult size head (approx. 19 in. / 48 cm to 22 in. / 56 cm).

YARN

A: Malabrigo Rios, Pearl (100 g / 200 yd. / 183 m)

Or other worsted weight yarn (#4).

NEEDLES

- US size 5 / 3.75 mm, 16 in. long circular knitting needles
- US size 7 / 4.5 mm, 16 in. long circular knitting needles
- US size 7 / 4.5 mm double pointed needles (DPNs)

Or sizes needed to obtain gauge.

NOTIONS

- Three stitch markers (two of one color and one of another color)
- Tapestry needle for weaving in ends
- Cable needle (cn)

GAUGE

With larger needles, approximately 9½ stitches = 2 in. in stockinette stitch.

With smaller circular needles, cast on 96 stitches. Place single color marker and join in the round being careful not to twist stitches. Work in k1, p1 rib pattern for approximately 4 in. for double ribbing (1½ to 2 in. for single layer ribbing).

Increase row: *p32, M1 purlwise. Rep from * around. 3 increases made—99 sts total.

Switch to larger needles and work chart from right to left beginning on Row 1, bottom right corner. Chart repeats three times around the hat. Use the two remaining stitch markers of another color to mark chart repeats.

Note: This pattern involves a lot of increasing and decreasing on different rows. The placement of the "no stitch" squares helps to visualize how the stitches in each row align with the ones above or below.

Switch to DPNs when work becomes too small for circular needles.

FINISHING

After Row 44 is complete, cut yarn leaving a 10 in. tail. Using a tapestry needle, weave tail through remaining stitches and pull tightly to close circle. Pull the tail to the inside and weave in all ends.

Block as desired. See page 12 for wet blocking technique.

Go on adventures!

KEY

 No Stitch

Note: The "no stitch" squares represent the stitches that were lost due to decreases earlier in the project. Do not skip a stitch. Simply treat the squares as if they do not exist.

Knit
k

Purl
p

(Knit, yarnover, knit) in 1
(k, yo, k) in 1

Purl 2 Together
p2tog

Knit 3 Together
k3tog

Purl 3 Together
p3tog

1/1 Right Purl Cable
1/1 rpc
S1 to cn, hold in back, k1; p1 from cn

1/1 Left Purl Cable
1/1 lpc
S1 to cn, hold in front, p1; k1 from cn

Knit Front, Slip Back
kfsb
Knit the stitch without transferring to right needle. Insert needle in back leg, slip both to right needle.

Make 1 Purlwise
M1p
Inserting left needle from back to front, lift strand between stitch just worked and the next stitch. Purl through front of this strand.

Mount Rainier

WASHINGTON

At 14,400 feet, the peak of majestic Mount Rainier is covered with snow year-round, even during summer when thousands of colorful wildflowers bloom in the meadows below. This beanie captures this beautiful scene in a vibrant Fair Isle pattern using seven different colors.

SIZE

One size fits an average adult size head (approx. 19 in. / 48 cm to 22 in. / 56 cm).

YARN

- **A:** Malabrigo Rios, Ivy (33 g / 66 yd. / 60 m)
- **B:** Stunning String Legacy Worsted, Fading Sunlight (<10 g / 20 yd. / 18 m)
- **C:** Stunning String Legacy Worsted, Big Sky (<10 g / 20 yd. / 18 m)
- **D:** Stunning String Legacy Worsted, Field Flowers (<10 g / 20 yd. / 18 m)
- **E:** Stunning String Legacy Worsted, Deep Forest (12 g / 24 yd. / 22 m)
- **F:** Malabrigo Rios, Plomo (25 g / 50 yd. / 46 m)
- **G:** Malabrigo Rios, Natural (33 g / 66 yd. / 60 m)

Or other worsted weight (#4) yarn in seven colors.

NEEDLES

- US size 5 / 3.75 mm, 16 in. long circular knitting needles
- US size 7 / 4.5 mm, 16 in. long circular knitting needles
- US size 7 / 4.5 mm double pointed needles (DPNs)

Or sizes needed to obtain gauge.

Continued on next page

NOTIONS

- Four stitch markers (three of one color and one of another color)
- Tapestry needle for weaving in ends

GAUGE

With larger needles, approximately 9 stitches = 2 in. in stockinette stitch.

With color A and smaller circular needles, cast on 96 stitches. Place single color marker and join in the round being careful not to twist stitches. Work k1, p1 rib pattern for approximately 1½ to 2 in.

Switch to larger needles and work chart from right to left beginning on Row 1, bottom right corner. Chart repeats four times around the hat. Use the three remaining stitch markers of another color to mark chart repeats.

Note: In order to avoid long "floats" (strands of yarn on the inside of the hat) do not carry a color more than three to four stitches without twisting the colors around each other in the back of work.

Switch to DPNs when work becomes too small for circular needles.

FINISHING

After Row 45 is complete, cut yarn leaving a 10 in. tail. Using a tapestry needle, weave tail through remaining stitches and pull tightly to close circle. Pull the tail to the inside and weave in all ends.

Use color G to make a pom-pom using your favorite method. Sew to the top of the hat.

Block as desired. See page 12 for wet blocking technique.

Go on adventures!

KEY

▨	A
☐	B
▨	C
▨	D
▨	E
▨	F
☐	G
☐	Knit k
◩	Knit 2 Together k2tog
■	No Stitch

Note: The "no stitch" squares represent the stitches that were lost due to decreases earlier in the project. Do not skip a stitch. Simply treat the squares as if they do not exist.

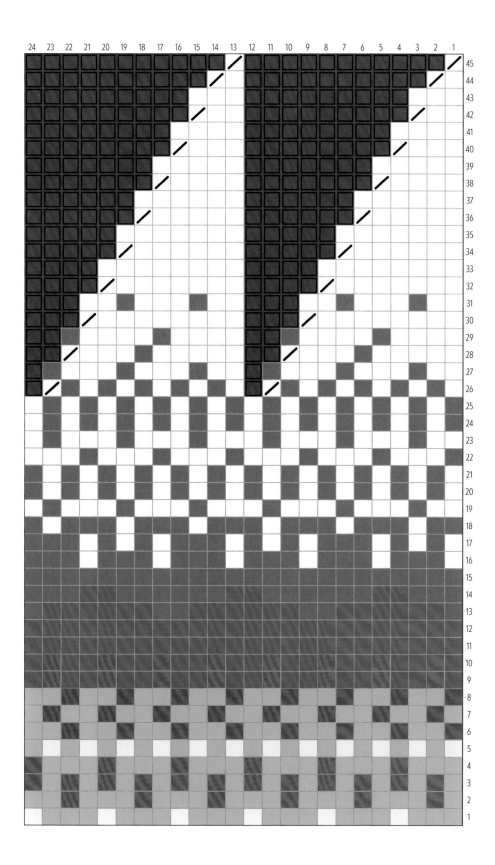

North Cascades

WASHINGTON

Jagged snow-covered mountain peaks, high meadows, wildflowers, forested valleys, and over 300 glaciers have earned this park the nickname American Alps. It's the only place like it in the United States outside of Alaska. Melting snow and rainfall feed the hundreds of lakes, rivers, streams, and flowing cascades (the park's namesake) while runoff from glaciers deposits a type of silt that gives the lakes of North Cascades their charactestic milky turquoise color. In this design, simple stranded colorwork takes you from the meadows, to the trees, to the cerulean lakes and up to the melting glaciers and snowfields that feed them.

SIZE

One size fits an average adult size head (approx. 19 in. / 48 cm to 22 in. / 56 cm).

YARN

A: Stunning String Legacy Worsted, Deep Forest (33 g / 66 yd. / 60 m)

B: Stunning String Legacy Worsted, Goldenrod (4 g / 8 yd. / 7 m)

C: Aly Bee Workshop Merino Worsted, Raspberry Ice (4 g / 8 yd. / 7 m)

D: Peekaboo Yarns Merino Worsted, Pacific (17 g / 35 yd. / 32 m)

E: Malabrigo Rios, Cirrus Gray (17 g / 35 yd. / 32 m)

F: Malabrigo Rios, Natural (20 g / 40 yd. / 37 m)

Or other worsted weight (#4) yarn in six colors.

NEEDLES

- US size 5 / 3.75 mm, 16 in. long circular knitting needles
- US size 7 / 4.5 mm, 16" long circular knitting needles
- US size 7 / 4.5 mm double pointed needles (DPNs)

Or sizes needed to obtain gauge.

Continued on next page

NOTIONS

- Three stitch markers (two of one color and one of another color)
- Tapestry needle for weaving in ends

GAUGE

With larger needles, approximately 9½ stitches = 2 in. in stockinette stitch, blocked.

With color A and smaller circular needles, cast on 96 stitches. Place single color marker and join in the round being careful not to twist stitches. Work k1, p1 rib pattern for approximately 1½ to 2 in.

Switch to larger needles and work chart from right to left beginning on Row 1, bottom right corner. Chart repeats

three times around the hat. Use the two remaining stitch markers of another color to mark chart repeats.

Note: In order to avoid long "floats" (strands of yarn on the inside of the hat) do not carry a color more than three to four stitches without twisting the colors around each other in the back of work.

Switch to DPNs when work becomes too small for circular needles.

FINISHING

After Row 45 is complete, cut yarn leaving a 10 in. tail. Using a tapestry needle, weave tail through remaining stitches and pull tightly to close circle. Pull the tail to the inside and weave in all ends.

Block as desired. See page 12 for wet blocking technique.

Go on adventures!

KEY

■	A
□	B
■	C
■	D
■	E
□	F
□	Knit k
⧄	Knit 2 Together k2tog
⧅	Slip Slip Knit ssk
■	No Stitch

Note: The "no stitch" squares represent the stitches that were lost due to decreases earlier in the project. Do not skip a stitch. Simply treat the squares as if they do not exist.

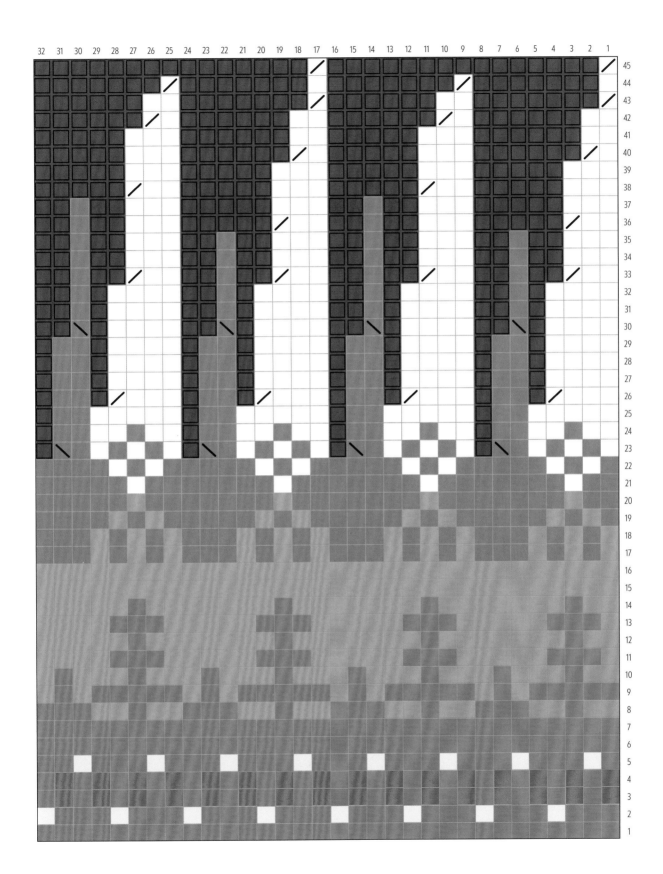

Olympic

WASHINGTON

The ferns, mosses, and lichens of the Hoh Rain Forest in Olympic National Park cover nearly every surface, creating the most vibrant green forest floors and tree canopies. Every rock, branch, tree trunk, or bench along the way becomes one with the forest in a setting of green so intense, it looks like it's straight out of a fairytale. This pattern creates an organic landscape of stitches meandering their way from the ribbing to the top of the beanie.

SIZE

One size fits an average adult size head (approx. 19 in. / 48 cm to 22 in. / 56 cm).

YARN

A: Malabrigo Rios, Lettuce (100 g / 200 yd. / 183 m)

Or other worsted weight yarn (#4).

NEEDLES

- US size 5 / 3.75 mm, 16 in. long circular knitting needles
- US size 7 / 4.5 mm, 16 in. long circular knitting needles
- US size 7 / 4.5 mm double pointed needles (DPNs)

Or sizes needed to obtain gauge.

NOTIONS

- Four stitch markers (three of one color and one of another color)
- Tapestry needle for weaving in ends

GAUGE

With larger needles, approximately 9½ stitches = 2 in. in stockinette stitch, blocked.

With smaller circular needles, cast on 92 stitches. Place single color marker and join in the round being careful not to twist stitches. Work in k1, p1 rib pattern for approximately 1½ to 2 in.

Increase row: *k23, M1. Rep from * around. 4 increases made—96 sts total.

Switch to larger needles and work chart from right to left beginning on Row 1, bottom right corner. Chart repeats four times around the hat. Use the three remaining stitch markers of another color to mark chart repeats.

Switch to DPNs when work becomes too small for circular needles.

FINISHING

After Row 47 is complete, cut yarn leaving a 10 in. tail. Using a tapestry needle, weave tail through remaining stitches and pull tightly to close circle. Pull the tail to the inside and weave in all ends.

Block as desired. See page 12 for wet blocking technique.

Go on adventures!

KEY

☐	Knit k
⚇	Knit 1 Through Back Loop. K1 tbl
╱	Knit 2 Together k2tog
⟋	Knit 3 Together k3tog
⟍	Slip, knit, pass skp Slip 1 purlwise, knit 1, pass slipped stitch over
■	No Stitch

Note: The "no stitch" squares represent the stitches that were lost due to decreases earlier in the project. Do not skip a stitch. Simply treat the squares as if they do not exist.

⦿	Yarn Over yo

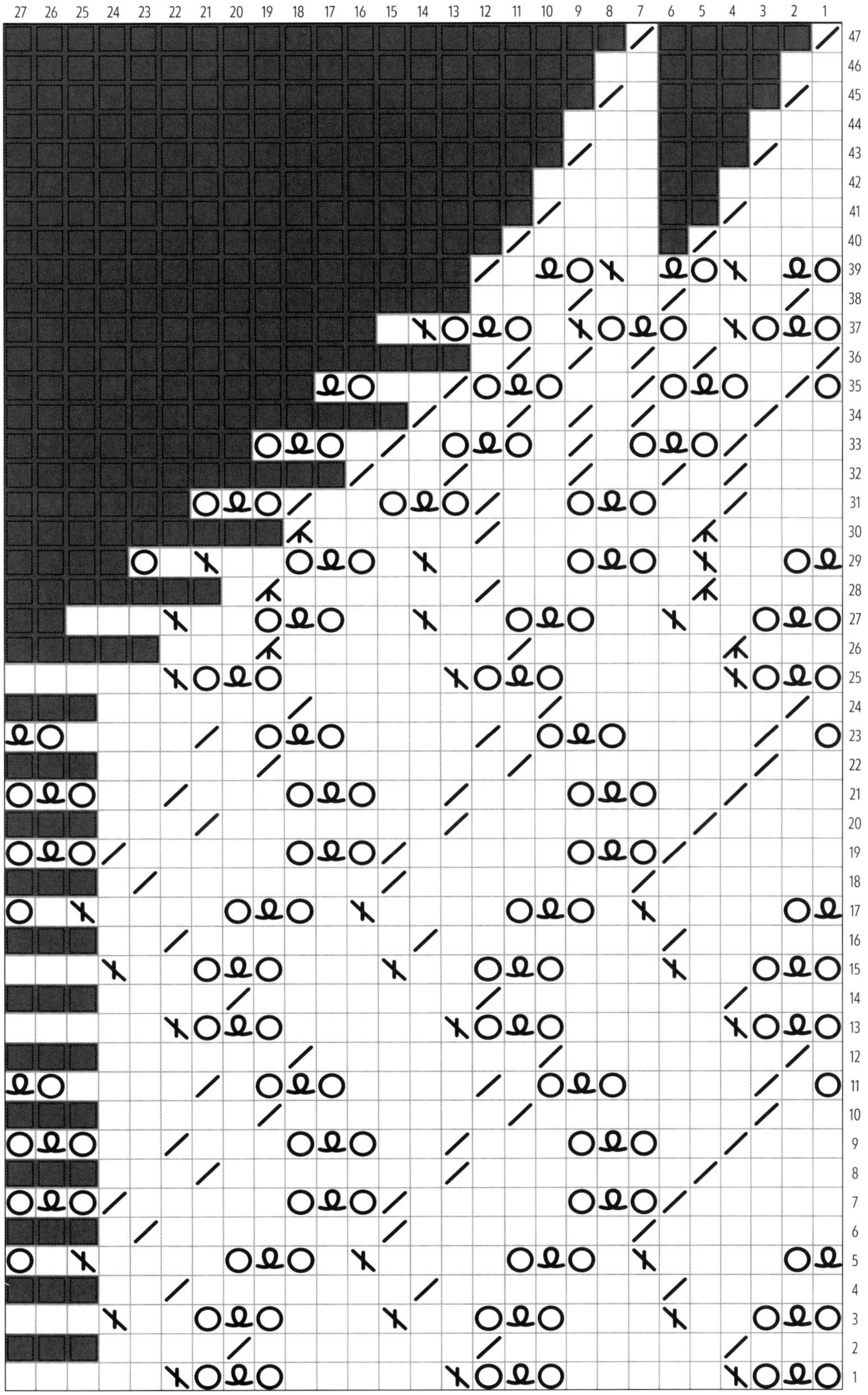

Pinnacles

CALIFORNIA

The main draws of Pinnacles National Park are the spectacular rock formations, talus caves formed by boulders falling on top of steep canyons, and a chance to see California condors. However, the sheer diversity of landscape and weather often comes as a pleasant and bonus surprise to many park goers. One day's adventures can take you from wildflower-strewn hillsides to exposed rocky vistas with a shady stroll along a cool stream in between. The color and texture of the rocks seem to change around every corner and even the weather can fluctuate fifty degrees from day to night. In beautiful but subdued colors of nature, this beanie features wildflowers, caves, rocky pinnacles, and a couple of condors—a design as diverse as the park itself.

SIZE

One size fits an average adult size head (approx. 19 in. / 48 cm to 22 in. / 56 cm).

YARN

- [ ] **A:** Polka Dot Sheep Whitefish Worsted, Moose Meadow (25 g / 50 yd. / 46 m)
- [ ] **B:** Polka Dot Sheep Whitefish Worsted, Huckleberry (13 g / 25 yd. / 23 m)
- [ ] **C:** Aly Bee Workshop Merino Worsted, Spooky (13 g / 25 yd. / 23 m)
- [ ] **D:** Polka Dot Sheep Whitefish Worsted, Barnwood (25 g / 50 yd. / 46 m)
- [ ] **E:** Stunning String Studio Legacy Worsted, Rocky Pass (13 g / 25 yd. / 23 m)
- [ ] **F:** Polka Dot Sheep Whitefish Worsted, Mystic (25 g / 50 yd. / 46 m)

Or other worsted weight yarn (#4) in six colors.

NEEDLES

- US size 5 / 3.75 mm, 16 in. long circular knitting needles
- US size 7 / 4.5 mm, 16 in. long circular knitting needles
- US size 7 / 4.5 mm double pointed needles (DPNs)

Or sizes needed to obtain gauge.

Continued on next page

NOTIONS

- Three stitch markers (two of one color and one of another color)
- Tapestry needle for weaving in ends and working embroidery

GAUGE

With larger needles, approximately 9½ stitches = 2 in. in stockinette stitch, blocked.

With color A and smaller circular needles, cast on 96 stitches. Place single color marker and join in the round being careful not to twist stitches. Work in k2, p2 rib pattern for approximately 1½ in.

Switch to larger needles and work chart from right to left beginning on Row 1, bottom right corner. Chart repeats three times around the hat. Use the two remaining stitch markers of another color to mark chart repeats.

Note: In order to avoid long "floats" (strands of yarn on the inside of the hat) do not carry a color more than three to four stitches without twisting the colors around each other in the back of work. Do not pull stitches too tightly or your hat will be too small.

Switch to DPNs when work becomes too small for circular needles.

FINISHING

After Row 46 is complete, cut yarn leaving a 10 in. tail. Using a tapestry needle, weave tail through remaining stitches and pull tightly to close circle. Pull the tail to the inside and weave in all ends.

Block as desired. See page 12 for wet blocking technique.

Optional Embellishments:
After all knitting and blocking is complete, use color B to add dimension to the wildflowers using single or double wrap French knots. Add as many or as few as you'd like. Using color C and simple straight stitches, add a couple of condors to the sky. See photo for inspiration.

Go on adventures!

KEY

▢	A
▨	B
▦	C
▧	D
▥	E
▤	F
□	Knit k
╱	Knit 2 Together k2tog
⩗	Slip Purlwise with Yarn in Back sl wyib
■	No Stitch

Note: The "no stitch" squares represent the stitches that were lost due to decreases earlier in the project. Do not skip a stitch. Simply treat the squares as if they do not exist.

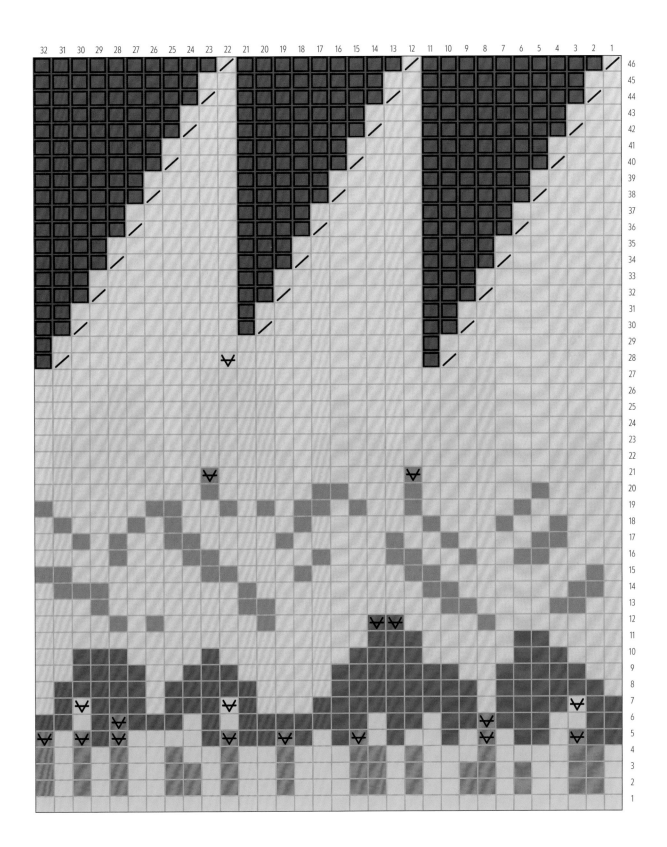

Redwood

CALIFORNIA

Gazing up at the tallest trees in the world is humbling, awe-inspiring, breathtaking, and even a little dizzying! Imagine looking up at a 35-story building, and you'll get the idea of how tall they really are. Found only in coastal California near the Oregon border, the redwoods thrive in the perfect mix of rain, fog, and temperate climate where they live for 500 to 700 years on average—some even up to 2,000! This beanie uses carefully placed rows of twist stitches to recreate the characteristic "twisted" bark of the redwoods while a simple vertical cable suggests the constant growth of ferns, smaller trees, and berry bushes that create the lush green backdrop of the beautiful forests.

SIZE

One size fits an average adult size head (approx. 19 in. / 48 cm to 22 in. / 56 cm).

YARN

Forbidden Fiber Co. Gluttony Worsted:

- **A:** Gillyweed (75 g / 150 yd. / 137 m)
- **B:** Butterbeer (50 g / 100 yd. / 91 m)

Or other worsted weight yarn (#4) in two colors.

NEEDLES

- US size 5 / 3.75 mm, 16 in. long circular knitting needles
- US size 8 / 5 mm, 16 in. long circular knitting needles
- US size 8 / 5 mm double pointed needles (DPNs)

Or sizes needed to obtain gauge.

NOTIONS

- Four stitch markers (three of one color and one of another color)
- Tapestry needle for weaving in ends
- Cable needle (cn)

Continued on next page

GAUGE

With larger needles, one "twisted tree" repeat and one cabled green repeat together should measure approximately 2½ in. across at their widest point (anywhere between Rows 5 and 24).

Note: Stranded colorwork, cables, and twisted stitches can sometimes cause work to tighten up more than usual. If you are a tight knitter, consider moving up a needle size for the body of the hat.

With color A and smaller circular needles, cast on 96 stitches. Place single color marker and join in the round being careful not to twist stitches. Work in k2, p2 rib pattern for approximately 1½ to 2 in.

Switch to larger needles and work chart from right to left beginning on Row 1 or 8 (see note under chart), bottom right corner. Chart repeats four times around the hat. Use the three remaining stitch markers of another color to mark chart repeats.

Note: In order to avoid long "floats" (strands of yarn on the inside of the hat) do not carry a color more than three to four stitches without twisting the colors around each other in the back of work.

Switch to DPNs when work becomes too small for circular needles.

Note: Be sure to twist strands behind a knit stitch or a "right twist" stitch and not a purl stitch. This will minimize the amount of contrast color that shows in the front.

FINISHING

After Row 55 is complete, cut yarn leaving a 10 in. tail. Using a tapestry needle, weave tail through remaining stitches and pull tightly to close circle. Pull the tail to the inside and weave in all ends.

Wet block for a better fit, especially if your finished hat seems a little tight. If your hat comes out just a bit too small, a little gentle stretching during wet blocking will help it fit better. See page 12 for wet blocking technique.

Go on adventures!

KEY

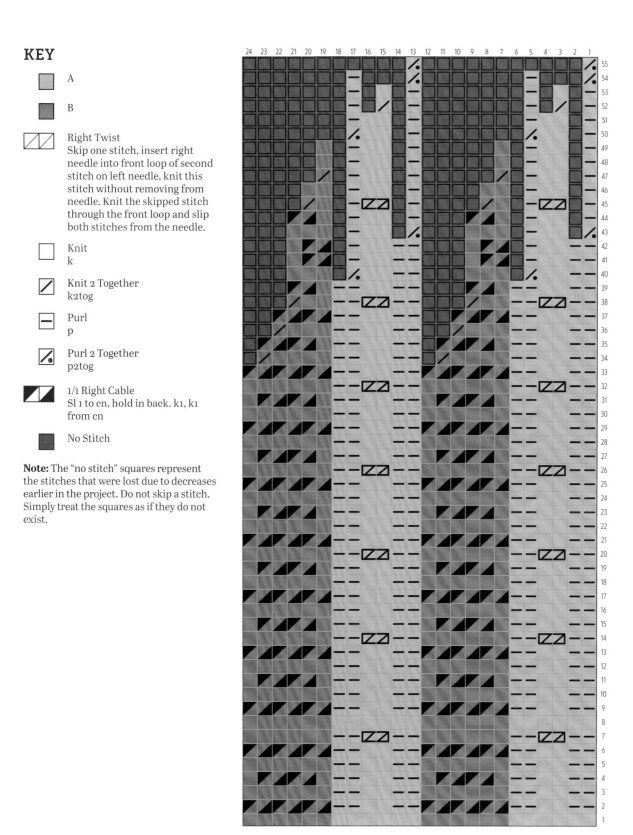

- **A** — (light grey square)
- **B** — (dark grey square)
- **Right Twist**
  Skip one stitch, insert right needle into front loop of second stitch on left needle, knit this stitch without removing from needle. Knit the skipped stitch through the front loop and slip both stitches from the needle.
- **Knit**
  k
- **Knit 2 Together**
  k2tog
- **Purl**
  p
- **Purl 2 Together**
  p2tog
- **1/1 Right Cable**
  Sl 1 to cn, hold in back. k1, k1 from cn
- **No Stitch**

Note: The "no stitch" squares represent the stitches that were lost due to decreases earlier in the project. Do not skip a stitch. Simply treat the squares as if they do not exist.

Important Note: For "regular version" (as shown), begin on Row 8.
For "slouchier version," begin on Row 1 and then skip Row 8.

Sequoia

CALIFORNIA

Walking among trees that are thousands of years old, several yards wide, and so tall you can't see the tops will inspire a sense of awe and wonder in anyone who sees them. These magnificent giants in Sequoia National Park attract visitors from all around the world. This beanie uses a vertical stitch pattern to create the characteristic reddish-brown bark of the sequoias while simple bobbles add a fun texture to the treetops.

SIZE

One size fits an average adult size head (approx. 19 in. / 48 cm to 22 in. / 56 cm).

YARN

A: Stunning String Studio Legacy Worsted, Caramel Latte (20 g / 40 yd. / 37 m)

B: Stunning String Studio Legacy Worsted, Rusty Gate (33 g / 66 yd. / 60 m)

C: Malabrigo Rios, Lettuce (13 g / 25 yd. / 23 m)

D: Stunning String Studio Legacy Worsted, Big Sky (13 g / 25 yd. / 23 m)

E: Stunning String Studio Legacy Worsted, Deep Forest (25 g / 50 yd. / 46 m)

Or other worsted weight yarn (#4) in five colors.

NEEDLES

- US size 5 / 3.75 mm, 16 in. long circular knitting needles
- US size 7 / 4.5 mm, 16 in. long circular knitting needles
- US size 7 / 4.5 mm double pointed needles (DPNs)

Or sizes needed to obtain gauge.

Continued on next page

NOTIONS

- Four stitch markers (three of one color and one of another color)
- Tapestry needle for weaving in ends

GAUGE

With larger needles, approximately 9½ stitches = 2 in. in stockinette stitch, blocked.

With color A and smaller circular needles, cast on 92 stitches. Place single color marker and join in the round being careful not to twist stitches. Work in k1, p1 rib pattern for approximately 1½ in.

Increase row: *k8, M1, k8, m1, k7, M1. Repeat from * 3 more times. 12 increases made—104 sts total.

Switch to larger needles and work chart from right to left beginning on Row 1, bottom right corner. Chart repeats four times around the hat. Use the three remaining stitch markers of another color to mark chart repeats.

Note: In order to avoid long "floats" (strands of yarn on the inside of the hat) do not carry a color more than three to four stitches without twisting the colors around each other in the back of work. Do not pull stitches too tightly or your hat will be too small.

Switch to DPNs when work becomes too small for circular needles.

FINISHING

After Row 44 is complete, cut yarn leaving a 10 in. tail. Using a tapestry needle, weave tail through remaining stitches and pull tightly to close circle. Pull the tail to the inside and weave in all ends.

Block as desired. See page 12 for wet blocking technique.

Go on adventures!

KEY

A

B

C

D

E

● Bobble
Knit into the front and back of next stitch two times, slip 4 stitches back to left-hand needle, k2tog two times, slip second stitch on right-hand needle over the first stitch

☐ Knit
k

/ Knit 2 Together
k2tog

− Purl
p

■ No Stitch

Note: The "no stitch" squares represent the stitches that were lost due to decreases earlier in the project. Do not skip a stitch. Simply treat the squares as if they do not exist.

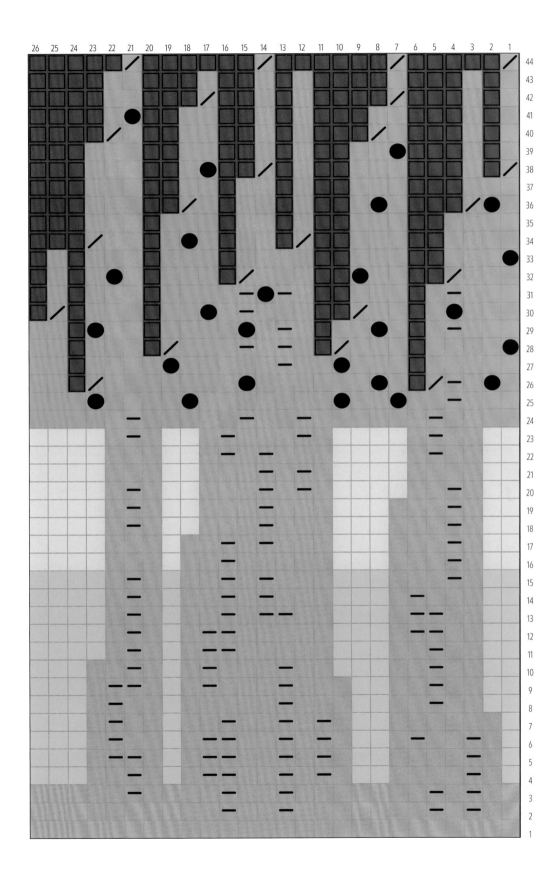

Yosemite

CALIFORNIA

From the tree-covered U-shaped valley and the granite cliffs of El Capitan and Half Dome to the majestic Bridal Veil Falls, this sweeping view of Yosemite Valley is perhaps one of the most iconic and recognizable scenes in all the US National Parks. It's truly spectacular in any season and any lighting. This beanie uses a simple textured stitch for the trees of the valley floor, while stranded stockinette stitch paints the rest of this remarkable scene. The optional waterfall in duplicate stitch is the finishing touch.

SIZE

One size fits an average adult size head (approx. 19 in. / 48 cm to 22 in. / 56 cm).

YARN

- **A:** Stunning String Studio Legacy Worsted, Dragon Green (33 g / 65 yd. / 59 m)
- **B:** Stunning String Studio Legacy Worsted, Stone (33 g / 65 yd. / 59 m)
- **C:** Stunning String Studio Legacy Worsted, Rocky Pass (12 g / 25 yd. / 23 m)
- **D:** Stunning String Studio Legacy Worsted, Cloudy Sky (25 g / 50 yd. / 46 m)

Or other worsted weight yarn (#4) in four colors.

Optional: Approximately two yds. of white yarn for the waterfall

NEEDLES

- US size 5 / 3.75 mm, 16 in. long circular knitting needles
- US size 7 / 4.5 mm, 16 in. long circular knitting needles
- US size 7 / 4.5 mm double pointed needles (DPNs)

Or sizes needed to obtain gauge.

Continued on next page

NOTIONS

- Two stitch markers in different colors
- Tapestry needle for weaving in ends and embroidering waterfall

GAUGE

With larger needles, approximately 9½ stitches = 2 in. in stockinette stitch, blocked.

With color A and smaller circular needles, cast on 96 stitches. Place single color marker and join in the round being careful not to twist stitches. Work in k1, p1 rib pattern for approximately 1½ to 2 in.

Switch to larger needles and work chart from right to left beginning on Row 1, bottom right corner. Chart repeats twice around the hat. Use remaining stitch markers of another color to mark chart repeats.

Note: In order to avoid long "floats" (strands of yarn on the inside of the hat) do not carry a color more than three to four stitches without twisting the colors around each other in the back of work. Do NOT pull your floats too tightly or your hat will be too small. Be sure to spread out your stitches on your right needle every five stitches or so to help avoid pulling too tightly.

Switch to DPNs when work becomes too small for circular needles.

FINISHING

After Row 44 is complete, cut yarn leaving a 10 in. tail. Using a tapestry needle, weave tail through remaining stitches and pull tightly to close circle. Pull the tail to the inside and weave in all ends.

Block as desired. See page 12 for wet blocking technique.

Optional: When knitting and blocking are complete, thread tapestry needle with 2 plies of white yarn and create a waterfall using duplicate stitch, half duplicate stitch, or any other free-form embroidery. Hot tip for the waterfall: Separating the 4-ply yarn and only using 2 plies at a time gives the waterfall a lighter appearance.

Go on adventures!

KEY

▨	A
▨	B
▨	C
▨	D
☐	Knit k
◲	Knit 2 Together k2tog
⊟	Purl p
▪	No Stitch

Note: The "no stitch" squares represent the stitches that were lost due to decreases earlier in the project. Do not skip a stitch. Simply treat the squares as if they do not exist.

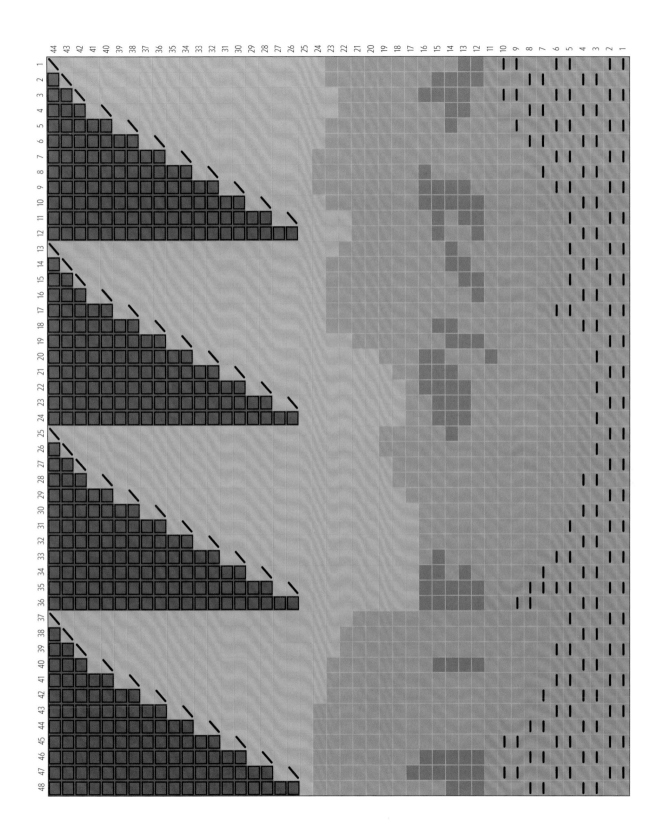

Denali

ALASKA

The seasons in Denali National Park come and go rather quickly. Well, three of them do anyway! The long cold winter of this Alaska park gives way to a short spring where animals come out of hibernation and green begins to fill the landscape. A warm and slightly longer summer beckons visitors from around the world while most of the park's 400 types of flowering plants show off their colors. The short autumn brings swaths of orange across the tundra while bears feed on the last of the berries before hibernating for the winter. Using nature-inspired colors and fun stitches, this design takes you on a four-season journey from a wintery landscape to snow-capped Denali Peak with the other three seasons strategically and delightfully sandwiched in between.

SIZE

One size fits an average adult size head (approx. 19 in. / 48 cm to 22 in. / 56 cm).

YARN

☐ **A:** Malabrigo Rios, Natural (33 g / 66 yd. / 61 m)

☐ **B:** Aly Bee Workshop Merino Worsted, Prickly Pear (13 g / 25 yd. / 23 m)

☐ **C:** Polka Dot Sheep Whitefish Worsted, Spinel (20 g / 40 yd. / 37 m)

☐ **D:** Aly Bee Workshop Merino Worsted, Pumpkin Spice (17 g / 35 yd. / 32 m)

☐ **E:** Malabrigo Rios, Plomo (17 g / 35 yd. / 32 m)

Or other worsted weight yarn (#4) in five colors.

NEEDLES

- US size 5 / 3.75 mm, 16 in. long circular knitting needles
- US size 7 / 4.5 mm, 16 in. long circular knitting needles
- US size 7 / 4.5 mm double pointed needles (DPNs)

Or sizes needed to obtain gauge.

Continued on next page

NOTIONS

- Three stitch markers (two of one color and one of another color)
- Tapestry needle for weaving in ends

GAUGE

With larger needles, approximately 9½ stitches = 2 in. in stockinette stitch, blocked.

With color A and smaller circular needles, cast on 96 stitches. Place single color marker and join in the round being careful not to twist stitches. Work in k1, p1 rib pattern for approximately 1½ in.

Switch to larger needles and work chart from right to left beginning on Row 1, bottom right corner. Chart repeats three times around the hat. Use the two remaining stitch markers of another color to mark chart repeats.

SPECIAL INSTRUCTIONS FOR ROWS 10–17

At end of **Row 9**, remove marker, slip first 2 stitches to right needle with yarn in back, replace marker to mark new beginning of **Row 10**. Work row as shown.

Row 11: Work row as shown.

Row 12: Work row as shown to last 2 stitches. Slip these stitches to right needle (with yarn in back). Remove marker.

Slip 2 stitches back to left needle. Replace marker to mark new beginning of next round.

Row 13–16: Work rows as shown.

Row 17: Work row as shown to last stitch, slip stitch to right needle, remove marker, slip stitch back to left needle, replace marker to mark new beginning of next round.

Work **Row 18** and remainder of chart as shown.

Switch to DPNs when work becomes too small for circular needles.

FINISHING

After Row 46 is complete, cut yarn leaving a 10 in. tail. Using a tapestry needle, weave tail through remaining stitches and pull tightly to close circle. Pull the tail to the inside and weave in all ends.

Block as desired. See page 12 for wet blocking technique.

Go on adventures!

KEY

☐	A
◻	B
◻	C
◻	D
■	E
☐	Knit k
⤓	Knit Strand Below Place right needle from front to back under loop formed by slip 3 below. Knit the loop and the next stitch together.
╱	Knit 2 Together k2tog
⊟	Purl p
⋁	Slip stitch with yarn in front. Do not pull too tightly sl wyif
■	No Stitch

Note: The "no stitch" squares represent the stitches that were lost due to decreases earlier in the project. Do not skip a stitch. Simply treat the squares as if they do not exist.

Note: Rounds 10, 14, and 18 are worked using color B only. You'll be knitting with color B and slipping color C. This creates a strand in the front of the work that will be picked up in a later round.

Gates of the Arctic

ALASKA

Located entirely above the Arctic Circle, Gates of the Arctic is the northernmost of all the national parks and one of the least visited. With no trails, roads, lodging, or cell service available, only the most adventurous and self-sufficient visitors stay for more than a few hours. Snow is possible any month of the year. Grizzlies, caribou, moose, and wolves roam freely. Mountains, rivers, and streams seem to go on forever. On clear dark nights, the northern lights dance across the sky as a reminder of the beauty and wonder of this Alaskan wilderness. In this design, carefully chosen colors and a bit of sparkle combine with mohair to create the ethereal effect of the northern lights across the night sky just above the horizon.

SIZE

One size fits an average adult size head (approx. 19 in. / 48 cm to 22 in. / 56 cm).

YARN

A: Malabrigo Rios, Cirrus Gray (50 g / 100 yd. / 91 m)

B: Polka Dot Sheep Whitefish Worsted, Nightfall (50 g / 100 yd. / 91 m)

C: Aly Bee Workshop Merino Worsted, Lifestream (20 g / 40 yd. / 37 m) & Lana Grossa Silkhair Lusso, Lime Metal (6 g / 40 yd. / 37 m) (one strand each held together)

D: Aly Bee Workshop Merino Worsted, Esper (20 g / 40 yd. / 37 m) & Lana Grossa Silkhair Lusso, White Metal (6 g / 40 yd. / 37 m) (one strand each held together)

Or other worsted weight yarn (#4) in four colors.

NEEDLES

- US size 5 / 3.75 mm, 16 in. long circular knitting needles
- US size 7 / 4.5 mm, 16 in. long circular knitting needles
- US size 7 / 4.5 mm double pointed needles (DPNs)

Or sizes needed to obtain gauge.

Continued on next page

NOTIONS

- Three stitch markers (two of one color and one of another color)
- Tapestry needle for weaving in ends and duplicate stitching

GAUGE

With larger needles, approximately 9½ stitches = 2 in. in stockinette stitch, blocked.

With color A and smaller circular needles, cast on 96 stitches. Place single color marker and join in the round being careful not to twist stitches. Work in k1, p1 rib pattern for approximately 4 in.

Increase row: *k31, knit in front and back of next stitch. Repeat from * to end of round. 3 increases made—99 sts total.

Switch to larger needles and work chart from right to left beginning on Row 1, bottom right corner. Chart repeats three times around the hat. Use the two remaining stitch markers of another color to mark chart repeats.

Note: In order to avoid long "floats" (strands of yarn on the inside of the hat) do not carry a color more than three to four stitches without twisting the colors around each other in the back of work.

Note: No need to carry slip stitch color across back of work. Simply knit with the other colors in that row and slip these stitches as you come to them.

Switch to DPNs when work becomes too small for circular needles.

FINISHING

After Row 44 is complete, cut yarn leaving a 10 in. tail. Using a tapestry needle, weave tail through remaining stitches and pull tightly to close circle. Pull the tail to the inside and weave in all ends.

Block as desired. See page 12 for wet blocking technique.

Work all duplicate stitching.

Go on adventures!

■	A
■	B
▫	C
▫	D
□	Knit k
╱	Knit 2 Together k2tog
Ⓓ	Duplicate Stitch Add duplicate stitching after all other knitting is complete.
☒	Slip Purlwise with Yarn in Back sl wyib
■	No Stitch

Note: The "no stitch" squares represent the stitches that were lost due to decreases earlier in the project. Do not skip a stitch. Simply treat the squares as if they do not exist.

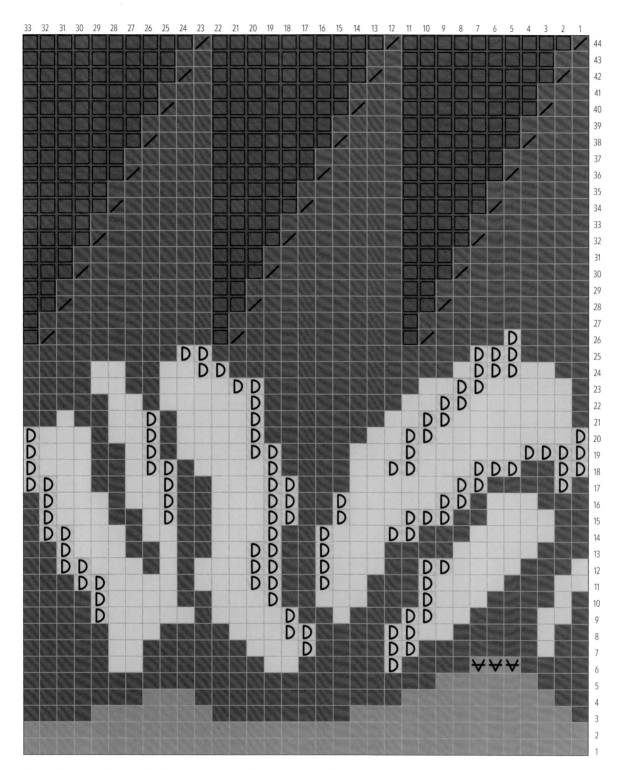

All Duplicate stitches: Work duplicate stitches after all other stitching is complete. In the meantime, knit these stitches using color B.

Row 6: No need to carry color A across back of work. Simply slip these stitches when you come to them.

Glacier Bay

ALASKA

With over 3 million acres of wilderness, Glacier Bay is filled with unforgettable sights and sounds for anyone lucky enough to visit. Calving glaciers, frolicking whales, and the symphony of songbirds in the rainforest canopy may be everyday occurrences in these parts, but experiencing them firsthand is a memory of a lifetime. This design features three breaching orcas surrounded by a bold design inspired by the beautiful artwork of the Huna Tribal House in Bartlett Cove.

SIZE

One size fits an average adult size head (approx. 19 in. / 48 cm to 22 in. / 56 cm).

YARN

A: Aly Bee Workshop Merino Worsted, Picnic Weather (50 g / 100 yd. / 91 m)

B: Malabrigo Rios, Natural (33 g / 66 yd. / 60 m)

C: Stunning String Studio Legacy Worsted, Little Black Dress (33 g / 66 yd. / 60 m)

Alternative Color Choice: For a different look, replace all blue stitches with another color such as red, yellow, turquoise, or green.

Or other worsted weight (#4) yarn in three colors.

NEEDLES

- US size 5 / 3.75 mm, 16 in. long circular knitting needles
- US size 7 / 4.5 mm, 16 in. long circular knitting needles
- US size 7 / 4.5 mm double pointed needles (DPNs)

Or sizes needed to obtain gauge.

Continued on next page

NOTIONS

- Three stitch markers (two of one color and one of another color)
- Tapestry needle for weaving in ends and working duplicate stitches

GAUGE

With larger needles, approximately 9½ stitches = 2 in. in stockinette stitch, blocked.

With color A and smaller circular needles, cast on 96 stitches. Place single color marker and join in the round being careful not to twist stitches. Work k2, p2 rib pattern for approximately 4 in. for a fold-up ribbing band or 1½ to 2 in. for a regular band.

Switch to larger needles and work chart from right to left beginning on Row 1, bottom right corner. Chart repeats three times around the hat. Use the two remaining stitch markers of another color to mark chart repeats.

Note: This is very important. If you are comfortable working stranded knitting using three colors at a time in a row, go ahead and knit all the colors as shown on chart, ignoring the "D." If you prefer to work with only two colors per row (as I do), you will need to duplicate stitch all of the color A stitches below Row 31 (indicated with a "D") after all knitting is complete. In the meantime, knit all these stitches using

color B and then duplicate stitch using color A. I prefer to duplicate stitch AFTER blocking is complete.

Note: In order to avoid long "floats" (strands of yarn on the inside of the hat) do not carry a color more than three to four stitches without twisting the colors around each other in the back of work.

Switch to DPNs when work becomes too small for circular needles.

FINISHING

After Row 46 is complete, cut yarn leaving a 10 in. tail. Using a tapestry needle, weave tail through remaining stitches and pull tightly to close circle. Pull the tail to the inside and weave in all ends.

Block as desired. See page 12 for wet blocking technique.

Work all duplicate stitches.

Go on adventures!

KEY

■	A
□	B
■	C
□	Knit k
╱	Knit 2 Together k2tog
D	Duplicate Stitch To be added after all other knitting is complete. **See Important NOTE in instructions.**
■	No Stitch

Note: The "no stitch" squares represent the stitches that were lost due to decreases earlier in the project. Do not skip a stitch. Simply treat the squares as if they do not exist.

Special Instructions for Row 27: Use color B to work k2tog on stitches where shown. Use color A to duplicate stitch over these stitches after all knitting is complete.

Katmai

ALASKA

O ne of the most iconic images of Katmai National Park is that of Alaskan brown bears catching sockeye salmon along Brooks River every July through September. Fattening up for winter hibernation is an essential part of the lifecycle of bears and is a spectacular tourist attraction for park visitors (from a safe distance, of course). With more than 2,200 bears in the park, Katmai is one of the best bear-viewing locations in the world. In this fun-to-knit hat, five wilderness-inspired colors come together in a classic design with images of bears, salmon, and trees. So Alaskan!

SIZE

One size fits an average adult size head (approx. 19 in. / 48 cm to 22 in. / 56 cm).

YARN

- ☐ **A:** Stunning String Legacy Worsted, Deep Forest (50 g / 100 yd. / 91 m)
- ☐ **B:** Aly Bee Workshop Superwash Merino Worsted, Prickly Pear (25 g / 50 yd. / 46 m)
- ■ **C:** Stunning String Legacy Worsted, Rusty Gate (25 g / 50 yd. / 46 m)
- ☐ **D:** Aly Bee Workshop Superwash Merino Worsted, Picnic Weather (12 g / 24 yd. / 22 m)
- ☐ **E:** Malabrigo Rios, Whole Grain (12 g / 24 yd. / 22 m)

Or other worsted weight (#4) yarn in five colors.

Optional Pom-Pom: Purchased faux-fur pom-pom

NEEDLES

- US size 5 / 3.75 mm, 16 in. long circular knitting needles
- US size 7 / 4.5 mm, 16 in. long circular knitting needles
- US size 7 / 4.5 mm double pointed needles (DPNs)

Or sizes needed to obtain gauge.

Continued on next page

NOTIONS

- Three stitch markers (two of one color and one of another color)
- Tapestry needle for weaving in ends
- Locking stitch markers (optional)

GAUGE

With larger needles, approx. 9 ½ stitches = 2" in stockinette stitch. Blocked.

With smaller circular needles, cast on 96 stitches. Place single color marker and join in the round being careful not to twist stitches. Work k2, p2 rib pattern for approximately 4 in.

Switch to larger needles and work chart from right to left beginning on Row 1, bottom right corner. Chart will repeat three times around the hat. Use the two remaining stitch markers of another color to mark chart repeats.

Note: In order to avoid long "floats" (strands of yarn on the inside of the hat) do not carry a color more than four to five stitches without twisting the colors around each other in the back of work.

Helpful hint: To make it easier to find location of tree placement later on, attach a locking stitch marker to mark placement of tree trunk on Row 3.

Switch to DPNs when work becomes too small for circular needles.

FINISHING

After Row 45 is complete, cut yarn leaving a 10 in. tail. Using a tapestry needle, weave tail through remaining stitches and pull tightly to close circle. Pull the tail to the inside and weave in all ends.

Block as desired. See page 12 for wet blocking technique.

Duplicate stitch trees: After all knitting and weaving in ends is complete, you will need to use Duplicate Stitch to create three trees as shown on the chart. You can work your trees in whatever order you'd like. I start with the trunk working from the bottom up. Then I work one side of the branches from the top down, and the other side from the bottom up.

Optional: Attach purchased faux fur pom-pom.

Go on adventures!

KEY

▨	A
▨	B
▪	C
▨	D
▢	E
☐	Knit k
◪	Knit 2 Together k2tog
D	Duplicate Stitch To be added after all other knitting is complete. See note under chart.
■	No Stitch

Note: The "no stitch" squares represent the stitches that were lost due to decreases earlier in the project. Do not skip a stitch. Simply treat the squares as if they do not exist.

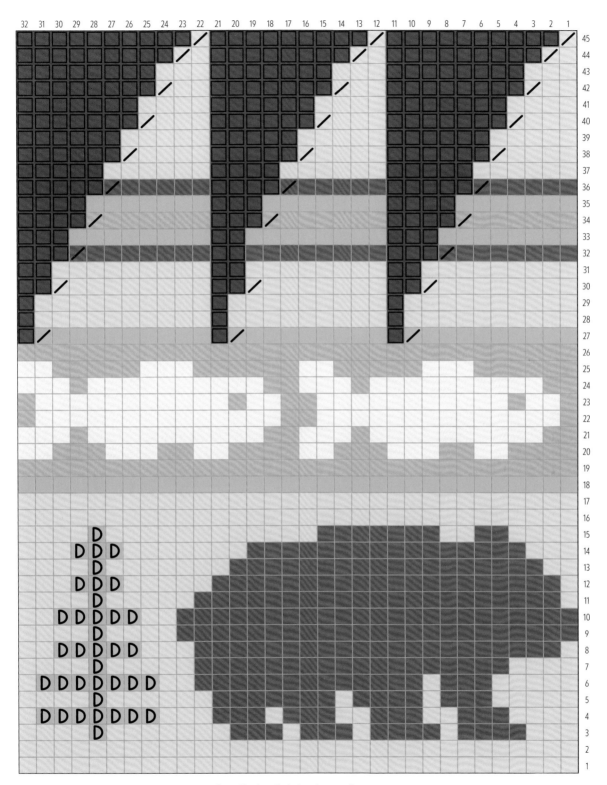

Duplicate Stitch: To be added in Color A after all other knitting is complete.
While you are knitting the hat, knit these squares using Color B.

Kenai Fjords

ALASKA

The smallest of the Alaskan national parks, Kenai Fjords contains the massive Harding Icefield which feeds dozens of glaciers throughout the park. Many of these glaciers meet the sea, creating the iconic and unforgettable image of massive chunks of cyan-hued ice breaking off into the teal blue water of the Gulf of Alaska. As these glacier chunks continue to melt and break apart, they create thousands of icy chunks in a speckled sea. This beanie uses textured and vertical stitches, beautiful custom dyed colors, and just a touch of stranded colorwork to recreate this icy landscape.

SIZE

One size fits an average adult size head (approx. 19 in. / 48 cm to 22 in. / 56 cm).

YARN

Peekaboo Yarns Merino Worsted:

A: Aialik Bay (50 g / 100 yd. / 91 m)

B: Bear Glacier (50 g / 100 yd. / 91 m)

Or other worsted weight yarn (#4) in two colors.

NEEDLES

- US size 5 / 3.75 mm, 16 in. long circular knitting needles
- US size 7 / 4.5 mm, 16 in. long circular knitting needles
- US size 7 / 4.5 mm double pointed needles (DPNs)

Or sizes needed to obtain gauge.

NOTIONS

- Three stitch markers (two of one color and one of another color)
- Tapestry needle for weaving in ends

GAUGE

With larger needles, approximately 9½ stitches = 2 in. in stockinette stitch, blocked.

With color A and smaller circular needles, cast on 96 stitches. Place single color marker and join in the round being careful not to twist stitches. Work in k1, p1 rib pattern for approximately 4 in.

Increase row: *k16, M1, repeat from * to end of round—102 sts total.

Switch to larger needles and work chart from right to left beginning on Row 1, bottom right corner. Chart repeats three times around the hat. Use the two remaining stitch markers of another color to mark chart repeats.

Note: In order to avoid long "floats" (strands of yarn on the inside of the hat) do not carry a color more than three to four stitches without twisting the colors around each other in the back of work. Do NOT pull your floats too tightly or your hat will be too small. Be sure to spread out your stitches on your right needle every five stitches or so to help avoid pulling too tightly.

Switch to DPNs when work becomes too small for circular needles.

FINISHING

After Row 49 is complete, cut yarn leaving a 10 in. tail. Using a tapestry needle, weave tail through remaining stitches and pull tightly to close circle. Pull the tail to the inside and weave in all ends.

Block as desired. See page 12 for wet blocking technique.

Go on adventures!

KEY

■	A
□	B
□	Knit k
Ⓠ	Knit 1 Through Back Loop k1 tbl
╱	Knit 2 Together k2tog
╲	Knit 2 Together Through Back Loop k2tog tbl
─	Purl p
╱•	Purl 2 Together p2tog
■	No Stitch

Note: The "no stitch" squares represent the stitches that were lost due to decreases earlier in the project. Do not skip a stitch. Simply treat the squares as if they do not exist.

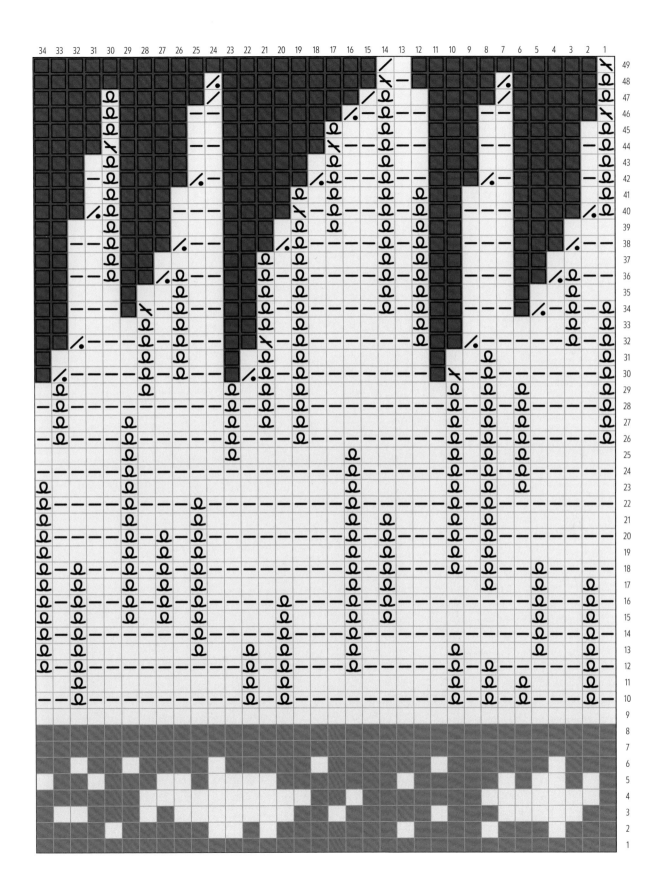

Kobuk Valley

ALASKA

One of the last great migrations on Earth happens twice a year across the vast tundra, sand dunes, and rivers of Kobuk Valley. Every spring and fall, nearly a quarter of a million caribou make the 600-mile trek between their northern and southern grounds, just as they have for 9,000 years—crisscrossing the dunes and swimming across the Kobuk River. With just the right colors and the magic of knitting, you can recreate this amazing scene. A couple dozen caribou will migrate across your hat in the spring and then back the other direction in the fall, swimming in the Kobuk River as they go, all with sand dunes looming in the distance.

SIZE

One size fits an average adult size head (approx. 19 in. / 48 cm to 22 in. / 56 cm).

YARN

A: Aly Bee Workshop Merino Worsted, Prickly Pear (17 g / 35 yd. / 32 m)

B: Peekaboo Yarns Merino Worsted, Zion Blue (20 g / 50 yd. / 46 m)

C: Peekaboo Yarns Merino Worsted, Warm Brown (17 g / 35 yd. / 32 m)

D: Aly Bee Workshop Merino Worsted, Island Sunrise (10 g / 20 yd. / 18 m)

E: Malabrigo Rios, Camel (17 g / 35 yd. / 32 m)

Or other worsted weight yarn (#4) in five colors.

NEEDLES

- US size 5 / 3.75 mm, 16 in. long circular knitting needles
- US size 7 / 4.5 mm, 16 in. long circular knitting needles
- US size 7 / 4.5 mm double pointed needles (DPNs)

Or sizes needed to obtain gauge.

Continued on next page

- Three stitch markers (two of one color and one of another color)
- Tapestry needle for weaving in ends and working duplicate stitches

GAUGE

With larger needles, approximately 9½ stitches = 2 in. in stockinette stitch, blocked.

With color A and smaller circular needles, cast on 96 stitches. Place single color marker and join in the round being careful not to twist stitches. Work in k1, p1 rib pattern for approximately 1½ in.

Switch to larger needles and work chart from right to left beginning on Row 1, bottom right corner. Chart repeats three times around the hat. Use the two remaining stitch markers of another color to mark chart repeats.

Note: In order to avoid long "floats" (strands of yarn on the inside of the hat) do not carry a color more than three to four stitches without twisting the colors around each other in the back of work. Do not pull stitches too tightly or your hat will be too small.

Switch to DPNs when work becomes too small for circular needles.

FINISHING

After Row 46 is complete, cut yarn leaving a 10 in. tail. Using a tapestry needle, weave tail through remaining stitches and pull tightly to close circle. Pull the tail to the inside and weave in all ends.

Block as desired. See page 12 for wet blocking technique.

Duplicate stitching: Work duplicate stitches where indicated using color E. These few stitches give each of the caribou more depth. I prefer to duplicate stitch AFTER blocking is complete.

Go on adventures!

KEY

▨	A
▨	B
▨	C
▨	D
☐	E
☐	Knit k
◪	Knit 2 Together k2tog
D	Duplicate Stitch Work duplicate stitches after all other knitting is complete.
▨	No Stitch

Note: The "no stitch" squares represent the stitches that were lost due to decreases earlier in the project. Do not skip a stitch. Simply treat the squares as if they do not exist.

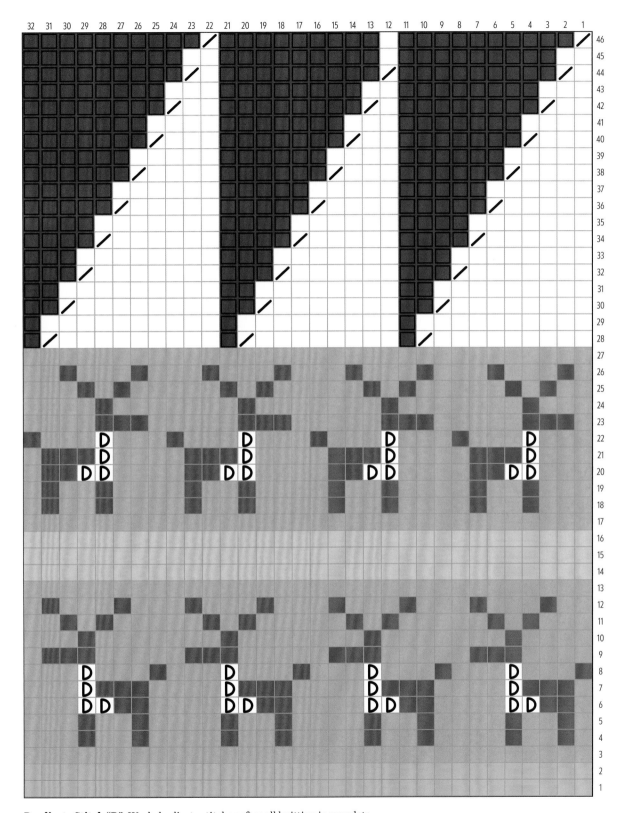

Duplicate Stitch "D": Work duplicate stitches after all knitting is complete.
In the meantime, knit these stitches using color C.

Lake Clark

ALASKA

It's been said that Lake Clark National Park embodies everything that makes Alaska spectacular: forests, glaciers, mountains, wildlife, lakes, rivers, history, great fishing, views beyond compare, and lots and lots of bears! Boaters on the lake often spot mama bears with cubs strolling along the shore. In the understated colors of dawn, the beauty and solitude of Lake Clark are captured in this beanie with a serene landscape of a lake, trees, wildflowers, and snow-capped peaks against a peach-colored sky. A few added stitches in warm brown hint at the presence of a bear family on the distant shore.

SIZE

One size fits an average adult size head (approx. 19 in. / 48 cm to 22 in. / 56 cm).

YARN

☐ **A:** Peekaboo Yarns Merino Worsted, Everglades Blue (25 g / 50 yd. / 46 m)

☐ **B:** Aly Bee Workshop, Merino Worsted, River Bank (13 g / 25 yd. / 23 m)

☐ **C:** Aly Bee Workshop, Merino Worsted, Prickly Pear (13 g / 25 yd. / 23 m)

☐ **D:** Aly Bee Workshop, Merino Worsted, Berry Punch (10 g / 20 yd. / 19 m)

☐ **E:** Stunning String Studios Legacy Worsted, Dove (13 g / 25 yd. / 23 m)

☐ **F:** Malabrigo Rios, Natural (13 g / 25 yd. / 23 m)

☐ **G:** Malabrigo Rios, Melon (20 g / 40 yd. / 37 m)

Or other worsted weight yarn (#4) in seven colors.

Optional: Several yards of warm brown to add duplicate stitch bear family

Continued on next page

NEEDLES

- US size 5 / 3.75 mm, 16 in. long circular knitting needles
- US size 7 / 4.5 mm, 16 in. long circular knitting needles
- US size 7 / 4.5 mm double pointed needles (DPNs)

Or sizes needed to obtain gauge.

NOTIONS

- Three stitch markers (two of one color and one of another color)
- Tapestry needle for weaving in ends and working duplicate stitches

GAUGE

With larger needles, approximately 9½ stitches = 2 in. in stockinette stitch, blocked.

With color A and smaller circular needles, cast on 96 stitches. Place single color marker and join in the round being careful not to twist stitches. Work in k1, p1 rib pattern for approximately 1½ in.

Switch to larger needles and work chart from right to left beginning on Row 1, bottom right corner. Chart repeats three times around the hat. Use the two remaining stitch markers of another color to mark chart repeats.

Note: In order to avoid long "floats" (strands of yarn on the inside of the hat) do not carry a color more than three to four

stitches without twisting the colors around each other in the back of work. Do not pull stitches too tightly or your hat will be too small.

Switch to DPNs when work becomes too small for circular needles.

FINISHING

After Row 44 is complete, cut yarn leaving a 10 in. tail. Using a tapestry needle, weave tail through remaining stitches and pull tightly to close circle. Pull the tail to the inside and weave in all ends.

Block as desired. See page 12 for wet blocking technique.

Optional: With tapestry needle and warm brown yarn, add duplicate stitch bears to the shore. See chart for placement suggestion or use your imagination.

Go on adventures!

KEY

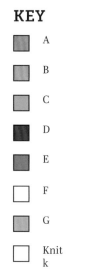

A

B

C

D

E

F

G

Knit
k

Knit 2 Together
k2tog

D Duplicate Stitch
Add duplicate stitching after all other knitting is complete.

Slip Purlwise with Yarn in Back
sl wyib

No Stitch

Note: The "no stitch" squares represent the stitches that were lost due to decreases earlier in the project. Do not skip a stitch. Simply treat the squares as if they do not exist.

Duplicate Stitches: Add duplicate stitches after all other knitting is complete. In the meantime, knit these stitches using color B.

Slip Stitches: No need to carry slip stitch color across back of work. Knit with the other 1 or 2 colors in the row and then slip these stitches when you come to them.

Wrangell-St. Elias

ALASKA

The largest of all the US National Parks, Wrangell-St. Elias is so massive, you can fit six Yellowstone National Parks inside its boundaries! Four major mountain ranges meet in the park, creating a landscape of peaks, valleys, rivers, icefields, and glaciers as far as the eye can see. As the glaciers carve their way across the landscape, scraping against mountains, they pick up debris and sediment, creating the stripes you see on the surface. From above, glaciers take on the appearance of icy roads winding through mountain ranges. Using only three colors of yarn, carefully planned colorwork creates layers and layers of mountain ranges atop a band of glaciers that resemble giant striped ribbons.

SIZE

One size fits an average adult size head (approx. 19 in. / 48 cm to 22 in. / 56 cm).

YARN

☐ **A:** Malabrigo Rios, Natural (50 g / 100 yd. / 91 m)

☐ **B:** Stunning String Studio Legacy Worsted, Dove (25 g / 50 yd. / 46 m)

☐ **C:** Stunning String Studio Legacy Worsted, Charcoal (25 g / 50 yd. / 46 m)

Or other worsted weight yarn (#4) in three colors.

Optional Pom-Pom: Malabrigo Rios, Natural (approx. 5 g / 10 yd. / 9 m)

NEEDLES

- US size 5 / 3.75 mm, 16 in. long circular knitting needles
- US size 7 / 4.5 mm, 16 in. long circular knitting needles
- US size 7 / 4.5 mm double pointed needles (DPNs)

Or sizes needed to obtain gauge.

Continued on next page

NOTIONS

- Three stitch markers (two of one color and one of another color)
- Tapestry needle for weaving in ends

GAUGE

With larger needles, approximately 9½ stitches = 2 in. in stockinette stitch, blocked.

With color A and smaller circular needles, cast on 96 stitches. Place single color marker and join in the round being careful not to twist stitches. Work in k1, p1 rib pattern for approximately 4 in.

Switch to larger needles and work chart from right to left beginning on Row 1, bottom right corner. Chart repeats three times around the hat. Use the two remaining stitch markers of another color to mark chart repeats.

Note: In order to avoid long "floats" (strands of yarn on the inside of the hat) do not carry a color more than three to four stitches without twisting the colors around each other in the back of work.

Note: No need to carry slip stitch color across back of work. Simply knit with the other colors in that row and slip these stitches as you come to them.

Switch to DPNs when work becomes too small for circular needles.

FINISHING

After Row 46 is complete, cut yarn leaving a 10 in. tail. Using a tapestry needle, weave tail through remaining stitches and pull tightly to close circle. Pull the tail to the inside and weave in all ends.

Block as desired. See page 12 for wet blocking technique.

Optional: Using natural-colored yarn, make a pom-pom using your favorite technique and sew to the top of the hat. A purchased pom-pom may also be used.

Go on adventures!

KEY

☐	A
☐	B
☐	C
☐	Knit k
╱	Knit 2 Together k2tog
⩗	Slip Purlwise with Yarn in Back sl wyib
■	No Stitch

Note: The "no stitch" squares represent the stitches that were lost due to decreases earlier in the project. Do not skip a stitch. Simply treat the squares as if they do not exist.

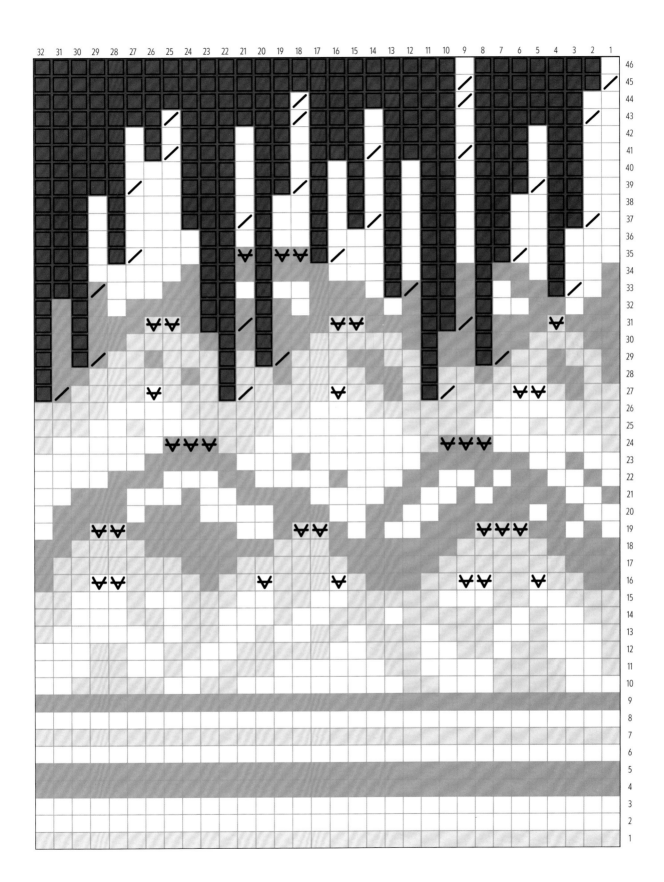

RESOURCES

Yarn Kits & Beanie Labels

NANCY BATES DESIGNS
www.nancybatesdesigns.com

Yarn

ALY BEE WORKSHOP
www.alybeeworkshop.com

ANZULA LUXURY FIBERS
www.anzula.com

BIG SKY YARN COMPANY
www.bigskyyarnco.com

CASCADE YARNS
www.cascadeyarns.com

DRAGONFLY FIBERS
www.dragonflyfibers.com

FORBIDDEN FIBER COMPANY
www.forbiddenfiberco.com

LANA GROSSA
www.lana-grossa.de/en/

LION BRAND YARN
www.lionbrand.com

MALABRIGO
www.malabrigoyarn.com

MANOS DEL URUGUAY
www.manos.uy/yarns

PEEKABOO YARNS
www.etsy.com/shop/
PeekabooYarns

POLKA DOT SHEEP
www.polkadotsheep.com

STUNNING STRING STUDIO
www.stunningstring.com

WESTERN SKY KNITS
www.wsknits.com

INDEX

ACKNOWLEDGMENTS

This incredible knitting journey through sixty-three US National Parks would not have been possible without the support and endless encouragement of so many wonderful people.

The core of my gratitude begins with my incredibly supportive husband, Scott, and amazing daughters Natalie, Caitlin, and Alyson. Thank you for adventuring and taking photos with me through the national parks and the pages of this book. Your countless reminders of "You can do it!" helped me believe I could—and I did!

A heartfelt round of applause and hugs goes to skilled tech editor, test knitter, and friend extraordinaire, Sally whose love of the parks and knitting is equal to mine. And to long distance sample and test knitter Donna: mountains of gratitude!

Turning nature into knitting takes a LOT of color. Thank you, thank you, thank you to dyers Amy, Alyson, and Tom for beautifully bringing to life the colors I pictured in my head and then making them a reality.

To yarn store owner (and everybody's friend), Molly, for the contagious passion, never-ending encouragement, and oodles of knowledge that she shares so willingly, I will be forever grateful.

Much appreciation goes to friend and photographer Eric Anderson, for his genuine enthusiasm and passion for great photos and creative shooting locations.

A huge thanks to my editor, Claire, for expertly and patiently navigating me through unfamiliar territory. What an adventure! And of course, none of this would have been possible without my publisher, Roger, who believed in this project from the very beginning.

Much love and happy adventures to all!

First Row: Lucy in Glacier, Nick in Gateway Arch, Lisa in Grand Canyon; **Second Row:** Sandra, Chris and Michelle in Yellowstone, Linda in Hot Springs; **Third Row:** Susan in Yosemite, Rosie in Shenandoah, Ryan in Death Valley; **Fourth Row:** Sarah in Canyonlands, Thomas in Kenai Fjords, Sally in Capitol Reef

ABOUT THE AUTHOR

An avid outdoor enthusiast, Nancy Bates has been knitting and crocheting for forty-five years and exploring the US National Parks for more than thirty years. She combined these two loves five years ago when the idea of creating a Joshua tree out of cable stitches popped into her head. She quickly became passionate about creating beanies for all sixty-three parks, and Nancy Bates Designs became a reality. You can find her at www.nancybatesdesigns.com, Instagram and Facebook where she encourages fellow knitters and park enthusiasts to share photos and inspire each other.

Originally from Canada, Nancy grew up in a family of eleven in the sprawling suburbs of Southern California surrounded by hills and open areas. With parents who nurtured and encouraged creativity and imagination, Nancy crafted, read, and explored her way through childhood, filling it up with as much adventure as possible . . . and hasn't stopped!

Aside from exploring the outdoors, Nancy's other passions include sewing, cross-stitching, painting, Dutch oven camp cooking (she once participated in a World Championship Cook-off), and occasional cosplay.

She currently lives in Southern California with her husband, two cats, a road trip–ready car, and a room full of yarn—with her three daughters close enough for family adventures as often as life permits.

weldon**owen**

an imprint of Insight Editions
P.O. Box 3088
San Rafael, CA 94912
www.weldonowen.com

CEO Raoul Goff
VP Publisher Roger Shaw
Editorial Director Katie Killebrew
Editor Claire Yee
VP Creative Chrissy Kwasnik
Senior Designer Judy Wiatrek Trum
VP Manufacturing Alix Nicholaeff
Production Manager Joshua Smith
Sr Production Manager, Subsidiary Rights Lina s Palma-Temena

Weldon Owen would also like to thank
Hilary Flood and Carla Kipen.

All beanie photographs ©2022 by Eric Anderson except
as follows: *Alyson Bates*: 26, 28, 78, 102, 106, 122, 144, 150, 154.
166, 168, 170, 180, 182, 184, 186, 188, 192, 200, 212, 220, 232, 260,
268; *Caitlin Bates*: 134, 136, 202, 204; *Nancy Bates*: 2, 4, 13, 14,
20, 30, 34, 36, 40, 44, 62, 64, 80, 90, 114, 120, 128, 138, 142, 190,
194, 196, 248, 272; *Natalie Bates*: 84, 104, 250, 252, 266; *Neel
Sutton*: 124; *Scott Bates*: 16, 24, 54, 156, 164, 176, 178, 208, 271;
Ted Thomas: 38, 66, 68, 86, 140, 138, 214, 238, 240, 242, 244

All location photos from Shutterstock except as follows:
Carl TerHaar: 75; *Don Geyer*: 207; *Henk Meljer Photography*:
187; *Jan Mulherin*: 259; *Kimberly Brewer*: 31; *Nancy Bates*: 15, 23,
35, 112, 143, 175 179, 219; *National Park Service*: 28, 76, 83, 167,
255; *Ron Wolf*: 203; *Wmpearl*: 139

Thank you to our models: Alyson Bates, Caitlin Bates, Natalie
Bates, Scott Bates, Kathleen (Missy) Billinger, Matthew
Billinger, Jenni Black, Akayla Brewer, Maisha Brewer,
Kate Cohee, Phoebe Graham, Elvis Herrera, Christine
Hoffmark-Coffey, Annie Hsu, Delanie Lutu, Desiree Lutu,
Karalee Martin, Emi Nomura, M. Gabriela Porter, Emily
Probst, Deborah (Sissy) Ramos, Richard Rios, Sarah (Sally)
Schultzman, Bobbie Soto-Billinger, Neel Sutton

ISBN: 978-1-68188-843-9

Printed in China by Insight Editions
First printed in 2022
10 9 8 7 6
2026 2025 2024

ROOTS of PEACE ⊕ REPLANTED PAPER

Insight Editions, in association with Roots of Peace, will plant
two trees for each tree used in the manufacturing of this book.
Roots of Peace is an internationally renowned humanitarian
organization dedicated to eradicating land mines worldwide
and converting war-torn lands into productive farms and
wildlife habitats. Roots of Peace will plant two million fruit and
nut trees in Afghanistan and provide farmers there with the
skills and support necessary for sustainable land use.